# SELLING SNAILS IN ISTANBUL

Christians living in a Muslim Land

## R K MUNRO

Edited by
RONALD CLEMENTS

Independently Published

# Contents

# Foreword

~

This is not the start of my story. My story began in 1952, and this account begins in 2002. Therefore, there is much unsaid. Maybe, in the fullness of time, I will work my way back from this point. The events I recount here only take my journey up to 2006.

I was born in a backwater town in the valleys of British Columbia. Ah, that's in Canada. I grew up with no illusions of travel or 'seeing the world'. Little by little, step by step, I left British Columbia and travelled to the neighbouring province of Alberta. There I met and married my wife Tülin.

When we married, we had no inkling that we would leave the shores of our native land and travel to places considered exotic.

So these stories are not a solo adventure. Tülin has shared the twists and turns that life has thrown at us.

Our first venture outside the bounds of the land of our birth was a two-year stint in the United States. This was a similar culture, with the same language - and yet it was different. We lived for one year in California and the other in Oregon.

Then, in 1980, with two children (our daughter was but 45 days old and had already accompanied us as we travelled across North America by car), we moved to Europe - our first fully cross-cultural experience. One year later we relocated to the land of Turkey. In 1983 our family grew by one more. As it says in Psalm 127[1], our quiver was full and we had received our reward from the Lord.

In time we moved to the Turkish Republic of Northern Cyprus and in 1987 we returned to Canada. In 1991 we emigrated to the United Kingdom.

Our children grew up and went out on their own. Our daughter returned to Canada, our oldest son moved to the United States, and our youngest has remained in the UK.

This account picks up in 2002 when we, as empty-nesters, returned to the Land of the Turks.

# September 2002 - A
# Small Town

All my Christian life I have read about Ephesus. And I have always been captivated by the ancient world. Reading of Mesopotamia, the pyramids, the Greek and Roman worlds intrigued me.

And now, a new phase of our personal chronicle has begun in Ephesus. Well, not the ancient city, but in its modern descendant, Selçuk[1]. We have left our life in the United Kingdom and arrived and settled in this small Turkish town.

The flight from the UK was too short for jet lag, and yet for the first few days, we were in a bit of a daze as we wandered the streets of the town.

Our daze, what caused it? Was it caused by the unfamiliar sight of so much sun? Or possibly the heat, which was more intense than we were used to in the United Kingdom?

Maybe our daze resulted from moving from a large town - and working in London - to a small Turkish town. Selçuk, on a good day, has a population of 23,000. But come winter and the off season, the population plummets. Those who can, return to their village or move to the bigger cities in search of work.

*Ruins of an ancient aqueduct striding through the heart of Selçuk town.*

Oh, did I say 'town', perhaps large village would be a more accurate description. It has more of a village atmosphere and village pace than that of a town.

Our last months in the UK were a chaotic amalgam of diverse activities and emotions. Our focus was packing and preparing to go. But we were still involved in the Sunday meeting and an annual Turkish family camp. We were breaking ties with a work and people who had be a major part of our lives for the past eleven years.

But now we are back in Turkey.

On our first Sunday in Selçuk, the weather was sunny and warm. It was summery, not oppressively hot. As we stepped out of the flat, we were immediately dazzled by the brilliance of the sunshine. Our hands snapped up to cover our eyes. This is one reason I wear a hat. I rapidly readjusted my hat to provide some relief. We turned left onto the street for the short walk to the church.

'To the *"church"*', my how things have changed in Turkey. We remembered our earlier time in Turkey, but that was twenty years ago. Then there were few Protestants and Protestant churches. In fact, there were about five churches in the entire country. That is just twenty short years ago.

We walked up the quiet cobbled streets past a few children happily playing with a ball. A little further and we passed the little kiosk where the local council sells freshly baked bread. The bread is reasonably priced and exceedingly tasty. At this hour, there were still people coming and getting their morning bread. It was nearly 11:00, but on a Sunday morning people do not rise early.

We came to a little mosque on the main road. The town is dotted with these 'pocket mosques'. They are small and crop up in the most surprising of places. Throughout the week they are mostly deserted. Even on Friday, the day when Muslims make an extra effort to go to mosque, these little ones are often empty.

We crossed the road and I looked ahead. The church building stands on a corner, not more than a hundred metres from the main road. I noticed a black stain on one of the window frames.

'Strange,' I thought to myself, 'that is some bad mould on that window.' I surmised there must be some water leakage.

In England it is common for black mould, especially around windows, to develop. Rain, damp and humidity are the norm in the UK. This results in mould, moss and everything green or black.

As we neared the front door, it then became obvious. This was not black mould.

Indeed, as I thought about it, it was actually highly unlikely, given the heat and long dry summer that is common in this part of the world. Someone, on that lazy Sunday morning, had risen earlier than most to throw tar at the two church signs. They were fairly poor shots. This was attested by the tar on the window frame, missing most of the one sign. On the other sign, the logo was obliterated. But the name of the church and the fact that it was a church was virtually unscathed.

This, I thought, was ironic.

If their intention was to frighten the believers, they missed the mark there as well. On that Sunday, there were two visiting groups. One group was made up of Turkish Christians doing a tour of the places in Turkey that the Apostle Paul[2] visited. The other group comprised believers from Moldavia.

The room was full, with extra chairs being required. The visiting Turkish group took the meeting. They led the worship and several shared. We were moved by the positive reaction to the vandalism. There was joy and peace that was infectious. We prayed for those who threw the tar. As Scripture says, we prayed for them and forgave them.

Our re-introduction to life in Turkey had begun...

A few days later, I was in town, sitting in a friend's car. The car was stopped by the side of the road and we were chatting with someone. The car, for no obvious reason, lurched side to side. It did this twice; two rather definitive, almost violent lurches. The driver looked over his shoulder, questioning if someone bumped into us? He saw nothing, nor did I. I, at least, assumed that somebody must have bounced the car for a laugh.

On my return home Tülin reported that as she sat at the kitchen table the rather large, 19 litre water bottle moved. And the wall moved as well.

The wall?!?

It didn't last long and she didn't know what to think of it.

Hmm, car bounces, no apparent cause, and our water bottle dances and the wall moves. These are not normal, usual occurrences for us. I wonder?

We checked the news and sure enough, there had been an earthquake with its epicentre in the Aegean Sea just off the coast from where we were. It registered at 5.4 on the Richter scale. We learned 5.4 on the Richter scale suffices to lurch cars, dance large water bottles and move walls…

We were reminded that this is a very active earthquake region.

As we began adapting to living, once again in Turkey and in a new town and in a new flat, I discovered we have a pet!

Well, that may not be totally true.

Ever since we lived in Adana in the south of Turkey, in the 1980s, we have been aware of these, uh, delightful creatures. Not harmful, *so I am assured*, and actually beneficial - or *so it is said*. Our flat is the proud residence of a wee lizard.

They eat insects (good), perhaps even mosquitoes (great). So we coexist. My only fear is that his natural 'defence mechanism' is to freeze. I guess, the reasoning goes, that by not moving, he would be invisible to me. Which, if I was hunting it, might be true. However, if I get up in the middle of the night - which is not unlikely as I grow more mature in years - it is then that I truly can see nothing. So freezing, staying in one place and not moving, may not be the best defence. The fact being I am not hunting him and I literally cannot see him. And in the middle of the night I really do not want, inadvertently, to stomp on him.

We have chosen to co-exist.

In typical Turkish fashion, our flat is finished to a high standard. It has ceramic tiles on all the floors. In winter, *kilims* are laid out for warmth. Come summer these said rugs are put away, allowing the bare tiles to help cool the flat. And in all seasons, this provides an easy to clean surface. The tiles themselves are white featuring a subtle grey pattern.

The kitchen and bathroom have ceramic tiles on the walls, floor to ceiling. You have a reassuring feeling of cleanliness. This helps ensure there is no mould or flaking paint.

The flat was basically fitted with all the basics, with the exception that there was no washing machine and no fridge. We borrowed a pint-sized fridge which meets all our needs. For our washing needs, we hand-washed. We will purchase a proper washing machine in the new year.

And so our housing was established, but we weren't there simply to live.

# 2

# September 2002 - Getting Settled

I t had just rained, a straight down, drizzly type of rain. I stood in our front room at the window and I realised the sound of a single raindrop on a leaf is almost imperceptible. But at the window, across from a small orange orchard, there arose a distinct pitter-patter of raindrops. It was loud and like the trampling of many feet. One raindrop, imperceptible, but multiply that thousands of times and it is something to be reckoned with.

About two weeks previously, we had a big thunderstorm. It was near to Selçuk, on the coast, over a tourist town called Kuşadası. The town is wedged between the sea and the hills. When this storm struck, cars were swept down the hills as roadways became impromptu river courses. In the end, the cars were piled on top of one another like so many Matchbox toys.

Getting a telephone line wasn't difficult for me - it was impossible. To begin with, you must have a residence permit - which we did not. So, it was the Lord — I didn't ask or suggest — that moved the landlord's wife to suggest getting the phone in her name.

We still haven't had the first bill yet. In the old days, when we lived in Adana[1] in the south, it cost $1000 USD to get a phone quickly. Our new phone was hooked up within two days. The hook up fee, I believe, was something like ₺13,000,000. Yes, I said thirteen million Turkish lira. That looks like a lot, but it is about £5.

Overwhelmed, I murmured, 'My, how Turkey has changed.'

We could have arranged for broadband in Selçuk. It would have been *satellite broadband*. The download from the satellite was at 512 kbps[2] - so that doesn't sound too bad. But, of course, how do you tell the Internet what you want to see or download? There was no direct means to talk to the satellite - it was a one-way street. So we tell the Internet what our request is via our telephone line. The speed of a dial-up connection is 56 kbps[3]. Oh, and even that speed was not guaranteed. It was often slower than that slow speed.

Still, on the dial-up system it took me the best part of a day to download a 1.2 megabyte file[4]. The connection kept dropping and it was very slow. This was a return to the old days before we spoke of 'broadband'[5]. So, satellite broadband sounds tempting. But the upload speeds aren't tempting. And it is expensive. Very expensive. In 2002, it would cost between £40 - £60 per month. That would be punishingly expensive. Ouch!

Starting over and setting up a new home, the question of transportation comes to the fore. We sold our wonderful Citroen diesel car in the UK. With what did we replace it?

I bought a pedal bicycle. It was new and cost me something like ₺170,000,000 or roughly £68. It is a multi-speed bike, with fenders — no mud on me, please. Oh, and I opted for a basket because I felt it would be useful, and also so it would look like a 'working bike' and not a toy.

I could have purchased a bike with suspension, front and back, for about ₺280,000,000. That would be about £120. Now, after riding my bike here, I wish I had gone for the one with suspension. The roads themselves are rough. But when I go onto a dirt road, then I really wish I had suspension.

∾

We did not move to Turkey for an extended holiday. I had been dabbling in making videos for several years. The barrier had always been computing power. But with every new year, computers were getting faster. Hence, it was now possible for more ordinary folk to make videos. Well, I am an ordinary chap.

It was for this purpose we came to Turkey. This was the time I would give myself fully to creating and making Turkish language Christian programmes. By selling the car, we had funds to buy a quality camera and a decent computer.

If you want a good computer, what do you do in a small, backwater town? Well, I rang up a place in the city of Izmir. Izmir is Turkey's third largest city and it is just an hour up the road from Selçuk.

The company had a salesman coming back past Selçuk. They arranged for him to swing by on a Monday night. He knew what he was talking about and together we defined the specifications for the computer[6]. This was limited to what I thought we could afford and included a UPS [7]as they are an absolute necessity here.

Then I spent most of Tuesday trying to arrange payment for it. I was happy they would take a credit card. This was how I had planned to pay for it. But they told me they would add a 4.5% surcharge to the bill. If I were to use my credit card, I would have to pay the seller 4.5% more for the card. Oh, and I would also have to pay Visa 2.7% more for using the card overseas. That would have added up to a whopping 7.2% additional, unplanned expense.

In the end, I took a cash advance and I still had to pay the 2.7% fee for using it overseas. The cash advance I paid directly into their bank account. Once they saw the money, they started work on the order. The next day, they arrived and set it up.

They didn't just deliver it and leave me with a bunch of boxes to unpack. No, they came down from the city and set it up! This was a great service.

So it is a 1 ghz[8] Mac[9] with two internal hard drives, one for the system and the other for video. But these technicians added a twist. They loaded the OS[10] onto both hard drives. So both the system drive and the video drive could run the computer, providing built-in redundancy if a drive were to fail. But they did more than that. They loaded both the old operating system, 9.2, and the new, modern operating system, called 'X', onto both drives.

They went out of their way and built in extra protection. If one hard drive failed, you could run your computer off[11] the other drive and still work. At least that was the theory. They said if I used Fire-wire hard drives[12], it would be even better.

# 3

# September 2002 - Our First Shoot

Our first video shoot was in Izmir — ancient Smyrna, about an hour's drive north of Selçuk.

It was only an hour's drive if you have a vehicle, er, and we did not.

An intercity coach would take us easily to Izmir. But we had a mountain of kit necessary to shoot a video. We decided the only alternative was to rent a car. We found a small place which let cars and much to my surprise the price was affordable.

I smiled.

It turns out that I'm a bit naïve in renting a vehicle; I haven't done it much. In the UK, it is pretty much standard stuff. Well, here was a reminder that we weren't in the UK any longer.

On driving the car to the flat to load it, it didn't take long before we realised that this was not like your typical UK rental car. The car worked and *most* of the basic features also worked, even if on a somewhat sporadic basis.

My smile had dimmed a wee bit.

So we loaded up the vehicle. And, by faith, we headed off to the metropolis of Izmir.

We began our journey by joining the otoban[1], also known as a motorway. It is mind-boggling how they have tamed the terrain, overcoming and spanning all the obstacles nature throws in its path.

My, how Turkey has changed!

We drove in relative er… I'm not sure how to describe our state. We drove to the outskirts of the city. Then we peeled off at a nondescript exit and made a left, followed by right and left, and so on to a road that we followed towards the centre of town.

We had a Turk with us giving directions. (This was in the days before in-car navigation via satellite.) I would say, without our guide, we would still be in Izmir. We would be lost in mindless circles, trapped within the Byzantine labyrinth of roads that make up the city.

'Thank you, Lord, for providing Ernie to guide us to the church.'

The Church of Saint John the Evangelist, Alsancak, Izmir[2]

A Christian band was doing a concert in the church and I had come to videotape the performance. I was hoping to create a snapshot of the ministry of the concert.

The group was from Canada and hence a long way from home. They spoke English, or was it French or both, I can't remember. Anyway, they shared their faith through verbal translation of the things said. They also projected the Turkish translation of the songs on an overhead projector,[3] and they gave paper copies of the lyrics to those who came. The people came to hear a foreign band and enjoy the music. And they were afforded an opportunity to understand the words of the songs as well.

The room was empty as the group went through their final sound check. Everything was as ready as the kit and acoustics of the room would allow. I looked around the starkly empty room and quietly wondered to myself where the people were for the concert. With just a few minutes to go, the doors were thrown open and people streamed in. I guess they were waiting outside the door.

Within a matter of minutes, the room was teeming with people.

With all the technical stuff done, the band and supporting people all retired to pray. This was not a rushed 'let's start the concert', but a real waiting on God. Quietly, they committed each other and the evening programme to God.

After prayer and returning to the main room, I slipped my shoes off and climbed up beside the main camera. This was to be my *first* time using the main camera in a real filming situation. The camera was an ex-demo professional camera. As I was just starting out, I realised the camera had far more experience than I.

I ran through a mental tick-list:

- tripod stable and balanced, tick,
- correct filter selected, tick,
- white balance done, tick,
- fresh battery loaded, tick,

- full tape loaded, tick,
- second tape ready, tick,
- mike turned on, tick,
- mike recording levels set, tick.

Everything was going according to plan and I was almost done with the tick-list. Then something caught my eye and I wondered, 'What's this?' A member of the band came over and asked, 'Can we turn the house lights down?'

I think to myself, 'It is important that this concert is the best it can be for the people who have actually come and to be here.'

I replied, 'Turn the lights down...'

But.

I have two cameras. One, I call it camera two, is a static camera. I have it set on fully automatic, so it *should* adjust okay. But the main camera, the number one camera, well, that is another matter. This is the first time I've used it in an actual filming situation. And it is all set to manual — *as it should be.*

Before we began, I had set the correct setting for the lighting. But now the lighting was dramatically changing. I hit the aperture button, and it seemed to cope. There was no time to attempt a new 'white balance'. And as the lights changed, so did the colour temperature. It was beyond my ability to correct that then. I was trying to adapt whilst things merrily carried on around me.

As the concert began, I started with a wide-angle shot. And now a myriad of questions flooded my mind: 'How is the sound?', 'What is the light like?' I did not like the light and I made a change on the fly... Was that a good or bad thing to do? The video looked better. But making the change whilst videoing creates a dramatic change part way through the shot.

...And, for the next two hours, I remained steadfast, standing beside the camera. I am trying to do my best, sore feet notwithstanding.

And, as time goes by, I try not to move too much. The last thing I want to do is to bump the camera.

That is how my evening went.

I felt, overall, it was a good experience. I learned a lot about preparation, camera technique, and lighting. And I was learning how to co-ordinate between two cameras. I thought and hoped that there may even have been enough good video to produce something.

However, the proof of this pudding is in the editing.

Our evening efforts at shooting the video were finished, but our evening was not yet over. We still had miles to go before we could rest.

After the concert, we loaded all the kit into our rented car and headed out to return to Selçuk. This time we were solo — no one along to give vital guidance. We entered one motorway, which led us to another. Then, unexpectedly, the motorway split three ways. Two lanes went left, two went down into a tunnel, and two off to the right.

What was going on here? I just wanted to go home to my bed.

By God's grace, I was on the right and was carried away to the right. The lane I was in split and carried me away - which was good as I wanted to go to the right.

Yikes! This was not fun.

We then merged with and joined another motorway. But we were separated from the main carriageway by a rather formidable metal crash barrier. There are four lanes going the same way and yet separate.

'What is going on here?' I frantically muttered to myself. Ahead, the two lanes to my left went up and over an overpass. And we? Well, we went down to the right, towards yet another motorway.

Not by plan, wisdom or knowledge, but we were on the right motorway to take us to Selçuk.

We got home in the end.

The fruit of our labour? What happened when the raw footage was loaded on to the editing computer?

Unfortunately, all became clear in trying to use the footage. The problems with the shoot I could not overcome. I could not make any kind of programme from the material shot in the evening. But I learned a lot.

My, how much Turkey has changed in the last twenty years. But we have changed too. It seems the only constant is that nothing stays constant.

There is much to learn, much to adjust to, much to unlearn as things have most definitely changed.

Regardless of where we abide, of new locales or old, there is another constant 'constant'. This is God's grace - His unmerited, unearned favour to us. His grace was clear when Ernie guided us to where we were going. And on our solo return journey, His grace brought us through the mayhem of motorways safely home.

We need God's grace day by day to live. We need His grace to adjust, change, and to learn as things around us change. And, as we have seen and felt on our return to Turkey, we need grace to unlearn, which is as important as learning. We want to be light and salt in this world[4].

# 4

# October 2002 - Landlocked Dolphins

It was September 2002 when we moved to Turkey. We went from the security of a full-time job to living 'by faith' in a sleepy Turkish town. I had worked with the council in a London borough and endured a daily commute on the M25 motorway. Selçuk is a small Turkish village in western Turkey. It lies close to the Aegean Sea and is nestled in the shadows of the ruins of ancient Ephesus.

The view from our flat was in a southward direction. In ancient times, the ground before us would have been open sea. But two millennia have passed. Even in Roman times there was a problem with silting. And silting, if left unattended, changes water into land. Today there is a broad, fertile plain.

The Temple of Diana was renowned as one of the seven ancient wonders of the world. Its ruin lies about 500 metres behind our flat. As the land around has silted and risen, the ruins of this once glorious temple now are in an excavated hole in the ground. Being a hole, it is often filled with slimy green ground water and is the haunt of a colony of very vocal frogs. My, how the mighty have fallen.

Ancient Ephesus, or the remains of it, is about a kilometre off to our right. That would be to our west, towards the sea.

The city has had a chequered past. Many times it has been destroyed and rebuilt. Even now, the village of Selçuk is its child. Many times it was brought low, literally, by earthquakes. At other times, it was by the hands of mankind as it fell to rampaging armies bent on destruction and pillage.

The excavated ruins are open to the public. These are the ruins of the Romano-Greek Ephesus of the time of the Apostle Paul. Here, in the grand theatre, the riot in Ephesus provoked by the silver-smiths occurred. It was here that Paul rented the lecture hall of Tyrannus and taught for many years. There are several *agora*[1]*s* in the ruins today. In one of these, possibly the large *agora*, Paul, together with Aquilla and Priscila, practised their trade as tentmakers.

Today there stands a plain where once would have been sea or salt marsh. Now farmers grow a variety of crops in the rich fertile soil.

In this region there are the ubiquitous olive trees. They grace the hills and uplands around the plain with a lush green cloak. However, we observe no groves on the plain itself. The plain seems to be dominated by rows and rows of apricot, peaches and citrus trees. Mind you, it is hard for me, a city boy, to know what is what. This is especially true as the season is early for citrus fruit and past the time for soft fruit – hence before us there is a veritable sea of thriving and flourishing green trees.

I have seen and recognised lemons – so I surmise that there must be other citrus fruit there as well.

On our strolls about the fields we saw aubergines, peppers and tomatoes. It was obvious as we passed that these fields are organic. Sometimes, a bit too organic, but we won't go in to that now.

A few days earlier, I was taking a contemplative pause. And I was gazing out of the window. The pastoral vista lay spread out before me.

Immediately across from us, just before the citrus plantation, there lies a small field planted with cotton. I know nothing about farming and nothing about cotton. Hence I do not know if it was a very productive field or not. But in my somewhat ignorant city-boy view, I noted the plants are quite low to the ground, ranging from about 80 cm to 120 cm in height. Maybe that is normal. Like I said, I do not know. But the field was white, as only a cotton field that is ready to be picked can be.

I noticed one or two women in the field picking cotton.

*Ladies picking cotton*

By their dress, I could tell these were village women. Their heads were covered with a white triangular headscarf made, fittingly, of cotton. The head covering was trimmed with either beads or sequins. It is essential that it is worn in a way that all the hair is covered. For clothes, the ladies wore sweaters or blouses. To complete their ensemble, they wore sleeveless knitted vests over all the other garments. These colours were dark; browns, tans, some navy. They were wearing *şalvar* — in English pronounced as shalvar.

To describe this garment, think of a skirt with trouser legs from the knees down. These were universally dark colours and usually of a floral pattern fabric. Finally, dark-coloured socks and plastic flip-flops. Flip-flops are not ideal footwear for working in fields where mud and snakes would not be unheard of.

In the heat of the day, the women take nothing off. Dressed thusly, they labour from morning through evening. Trust me, it is anything but cool here.

As I was watching, another woman suddenly appeared, rising out of the white/green of the field. She had been fully stooped over at the waist to pick the cotton and was not visible to me. She was hidden within the cotton plants.

Then another lady rose from within the sea of cotton plants. She was followed by another and another. Then one of the women stooped down and was gone. Once again lost between the rows of cotton.

There was no way of knowing where or when she would appear again. Stooped over, she would pick cotton, putting it in a sack she had tied around her, and she would work her way down the row of plants until the sack was full. Then she would rise and, from my perspective, surface. How you maintain that position and labour, bent over like that, is a mystery to me.

Watching the women rise and plunge out of sight reminded me of a school of dolphins or whales which, when swimming along, surface briefly and then disappear into the sea once again. The difference here is that these are women - the only man is the driver of the tractor. His task is to lug the bags of cotton. And it is his task to load the cotton into the larger bags. He can be a part-time cotton-picker — it is up to him. But he can often be seen resting under the shade of a tree. The ladies, however, spend the day from early morning, through the heat of the day, to the evening bent over from the waist, picking, picking, picking cotton. The small, preschool children play by the road while their mothers are in the fields. The 8 or 9-year-old daughters join their mothers labouring in the field.

The dolphins in the sea, when they dive beneath the waves, are in their element; free and sleek. Not so for these ladies. They are not swimming in the cotton. Their labour is unnatural, backbreaking and arduous.

Their reward, after all the effort and exertion, is almost enough to live on. *Please note the use of the adverb 'almost' means 'not enough to live on'.* Their reward for their perseverance and sweat is not enough to send their children to school. And sending a child to school removes a pair of productive hands from the family income and also costs money. Their hard-earned wages are not enough for the basics of life.

In the West, we take 'going to school' for granted. We think of it as a birthright or even a fundamental human right.

These ladies labour hoping to have decent housing. They are not looking for a palace, but something basic and dry. The lofty goals they aspire to is to have adequate food. They aspire, but many of them never see the reality. These fields are white unto harvest. But these harvest workers only share in the sweat, toil and labour. They receive precious little recompense for their labours.

They labour hard and long when there is work and suffer lack when there is none. These people have no practical or realistic hope in this world. All their efforts, all their toil, all their energy goes to survive today. There is no light at the end of the tunnel for them.

Death only promises an end to the pitiless labour in this life, but for them there is no assurance of acceptance in the presence of God. Life is hard – death is even harder.

For them, they have never heard 'For God so loved the world that He gave His one and only Son'[2] in order that they might have a fulfilling life here and the promise of a better eternity. Indeed, Jesus said He came that we might have life and have it to the full[3]. A full life is not a life with all the things we desire. He promises a life that is not bound to our circumstances. As Paul said:

'I know what it is to be in need, and I know what it is to have plenty. I have learned the secret of being content in any and every situation, whether well fed or hungry, whether living in plenty or in want.'

Philippians 4:12 NIVUK

And He promises to be with us until the end of the age. He is our help in our time of sorrows and His strength keeps us in the difficult time.

This is indeed Good News.

And it is to sharing this Good News that the Lord has called all who have 'tasted and seen that the Lord is good'[4]. Praise the Lord that He has given us this New Life.

# February 2003 - The Art of 'Crossing to the Other Side'

I n the twinkling of an eye, my mind flashed back. I could see the grass beside the road and the line of trees. Tülin and I approached the road. We were not at a corner, nor a zebra crossing or pelican crossing. We approach the side of the road, in the middle, part way between the corners. All the traffic in the street stopped. They responded to our position on the side of the road and they stopped to let us cross.

I was awestruck. That was in Alberta, Canada in 1987.

We weren't at a traffic light, we weren't at a marked, prepared or official crossing point. We had not even stepped off the curb. But our intention to cross was understood and the traffic took immediate actions to facilitate our crossing. That happened long ago, but it had such an impact on me I still remember it.

Now I stood at an official, proper, designated crossing point in Izmir. To my left there was a constant stream of cars, trucks, vans and buses flooding towards us. They were pouring down the three-lane road in five columns. The columns were not fixed as the vehicles twisted, weaved, manoeuvred as they sought advantage. They were flying down the road and intent only on getting to their destinations.

This, clearly, was not Alberta in 1987.

Here, it was clear, different rules apply.

Girding up my loins, I mustered all my deep-rooted skills as a hunter/gatherer. Tülin and I joined the throng of other would-be road crossers to engage in the art of *'crossing to the other side'*.

All the drivers know we know what we are to do. The onus is on us, we bear the sole responsibility **not** to step in front of them. We must not impede their forward progress. We may want to cross the road, but in doing so it is our task not to hinder them in their pursuit of their goal.

If someone steps in front of a vehicle, the drivers 'know' they will step out of the way before they pass that point in the road.

It is not their concern.

We, the throng, the gaggle, the gathering of young, old, male, female, healthy and infirm, are poised on the edge of the road. Before us flows the maelstrom of traffic. We are alive and alert. We are waiting, watching, judging the right moment to make the plunge. Each one is weighing up all the parameters. We are judging when to enter the fray and to act.

You make the first step. It must not be faltering, nor hesitant. We are crossing a road and we know what we are doing. We know where and when we are going. We cross just after one flying vehicle. Then a pause as the car in that lane careens past behind us whilst another flies before. Another quick step and we are halfway to the island of tranquillity amid the raging torrent of traffic. One more quick walk and pause and another and we have arrived. We are moving as a herd.

We carry on. The island of tranquillity is in the middle of the road. It is a safe place, but the job is only half done.

Trained up, adrenalin flowing, and all senses heightened - we feel ready for whatever the vehicles will throw at us. As a cooperative body, following the same rules, we step and pause as required. We, together, attain the other side.

I feel a sense of accomplishment, of joy, of triumph.

But here, it is clear, for crossing the road, different rules apply. In Alberta, local rules are in play and it works well. Here, different rules apply, and here too, it works. I will refrain from adding the adjective 'well'.

Having just returned to Turkey, we are the ones out of step. For us, it is a new culture. Things are different.

Whilst some things change, some things do not. The underlying principals of humanity do not. Things like honesty, integrity and truth are valued. These foundational aspects are found and are important in all cultures. The expression may vary, but the essence does not.

And a simple task like crossing a street can be and often is culturally defined. How you cross a street may be subject to change.

But who we are must and needs to be settled on a firmer foundation. For in life we are challenged to withstand the torrents of oncoming challenges that would seek to mould us into something we would not be.

Changing one aspect – like crossing a street – affords us life and peace. However, allowing a culture to change who we are and by what lights we live endangers what our life is about.

Adapting and change are essential in life - but making change knowledgeably is also required.

# March 2003 - 'Şey'

'*Şey*' said I.

The Turkish word for 'thing' is '*şey*'. The first letter is an 's' with a hook under it (ş) giving it the sound 'sh'. So you pronounce the word 'shey'. It means 'thing' but is used to communicate far more than just 'thing'. It is also used as a vocalised pause and as a substitute for something that you do not know. It is not strictly a Turkish word. In the early years of the Republic, when the language was being cleaned of foreign words, it was suggested to remove '*şey*' from the language. But, in the debate's course, one person asserted that at the Resurrection, all Turks would sit up in their graves and the first word they would utter at that moment would be '*şey*' . It was left in the language.

I am glad they did.

The man I said 'thing' to had a puzzled face. It was not a frustrated face as I would be if our positions were reversed. He rooted around and pulled a package out and showed it to me.

'No, not that "thing", more like, well I don't know the word for it, but, like "thing". It differs greatly from this, more like, uh, "thing"'.

Off he goes, scurrying through his shop, poking, prodding and otherwise trying to discover what this foreigner's 'thing' was. The shelves go from floor to ceiling and are artfully, artistically and attractively stacked with the various products on offer. There is not an empty space to be seen.

Another package is offered – again it is not the right 'thing' . I gesture with my hands, but I am not sure how to convey the meaning of 'thing' through hand, arm and facial gestures.

I try.

He watches intently. Is there a glimmer of understanding? Have his powers of interpretation been up to the challenge of my feeble gesturing? Off he flies, feverishly searching through the mountain of products, and at last he returns with a package.

'Hm, well', says I, 'it is like…' I am stumped for words. I add, not helpfully, 'more long, uh, wide.'

I am struggling. 'Er, I mean more with, kind of, protrudy.' I sum up by adding, 'Square in a round sort of way.'

While he digs around in the back, out of sight, I ponder the reality that although I speak Turkish and have preached for years, often I can be stumbled up by a simple, single word. The word may describe an item that may be common as grass or as rare as a diamond here in Turkey. It is not a word that I have ever needed before – but now I need the item being described. I have a dictionary. It is a great big, multi-kilo dictionary. It is a two volume set. It confidently declares, 'I have all the words you may want'. But it is on the long list to be brought to Turkey – it is far too heavy and bulky to make it on the short list.

*(This was in the day before mobile phones. These, we now say, are the 'old days'. With today's mobile phones, this would not be a problem.)*

The quest continues.

Time ticks on as we labour together to discover my 'thing'. After many gestures and dogged perseverance, the meaning of my 'thing' is determined. We have learned what my 'thing' is! Great!

But he doesn't have it.

And then he does a typical Turkish response. Now he knows what my 'thing' is, he knows where there is one. He does not give directions, he excuses himself, departs the shop, flies to wherever this source of my 'thing' is hidden. There he collects the item and returns to me. I am now the proud owner of my 'thing'. And after all the hassle and trouble and inconvenience with which we have graced his shop – he offers Tülin and I tea.

Tea is grown in Turkey on the Black Sea coast. And it is an essential part of all Turkish social interactions. It is a cheap, common beverage that is enjoyed by all and drunk in copious amounts. Whether in homes, tea shops, shops, anywhere that Turks are found - tea is found.

My new 'friend' in the shop has offered us tea. I accept – though now I must refrain from the two cubes of sugar that normally are added to this demitasse of delicious dark brown liquid. Tülin must refuse the actual tea itself. For her, it is a highway to a migraine. The shop keeper then offers Apple tea, 'Ilhamur' *Linden* tea, or 'Ada' *Sage* tea. She opts for Ada tea. We share the tea together and have a nice chat with our friend before taking our leave to continue the business of the day.

You might be tempted to think that the purchase we made that day was significant or large. But quite the contrary, it was minor and insignificant. Turkish hospitality is not linked to the magnitude of the purchase.

# 7

# April 2003 - A Castle, A Climb, A Turtle and a Twist

My eyes continued to drift from the road in front, to my left... to my left and up. There, standing proud on the crest of a low mountain with the clear Aegean sky behind and the dry, burlap-coloured hillsides like a skirt dropping to the base, a castle dominated the valley. In ancient times, this was a major crossroads. The roads from Ephesus, Smyrna, and Philadelphia joined in the valley at the base of this formidable fortress.

*Keçi Kale - Goat Castle, from the valley floor*

Who built this castle? When? Why? What is its history? Who lived there? My mind was flooded with questions and my interest was piqued.

My eyes were forced back to the road, where the dance of traffic really required more than my part-time attention.

This was the autumn of 1983. We had been living in Turkey for two years and were doing a tour. We were travelling from the ruins of ancient Ephesus on our way to the city of Izmir. Izmir lies on the ruins of the ancient city of Smyrna.

This was my first introduction to the castle known locally as Keçi Kale. Keçi Kale simply means 'Goat Castle'. Over the years, I visited Selçuk/Ephesus. Each time I would pass under this castle brooding on the mountain. The castle built to guard the roads below continues to gaze down upon the main highway - now a modern motorway.

In this way, my interest never waned and indeed, with each passing visit, increased in its intensity. Perched, as it was on top of the mountain, I yearned to visit it, to see it up close and personal. I wanted to look down from the lofty heights as many soldiers have done in time past.

I don't have a 'bucket list' - but if I did, visiting this castle would have been on it.

When we moved to Selçuk in 2002, I heard some believers had made the trek to the summit. Hearing this, my interest was transformed into a quest. But how do I get to the base of the mountain, it is some ten kilometres from Selçuk?

I learned that a visiting group of students from a Bible school in Sweden were planning on making the ascent. My immediate question - without thoughts or hesitation - was, 'Do you have room for two more?'

The response was a warm invitation.

So, a few days later, we found ourselves bundled into a crowded minivan making the short trip to the base of the mountain.

The quest was on!

There were 18 people in the group. As you would imagine, various degrees of fitness meant the one large group quickly broke down into several subgroups according to ability. Tülin and I were by far the oldest in the group and we formed our own little subgroup.

We had been told of a trail – and indeed there was one. It was composed of rough-hewn stones and following a serpentine path. The trail slowly wound its way back and forth across the face of the mountain on a gradual ascent towards the summit. In its heyday, hundreds of years ago — or was it a millennium? — it probably made the climb a simple and straightforward task.

Now, for centuries, the castle has been abandoned, hence the trail has not been maintained. In some places it was clearly a trail and nearly its full width. In others it was more a part of the trail. Bits were worn away, fallen away, or simply 'away'. Mind you, in other places, it was only by deductive reasoning and faith that the trail would be re-acquired after vanishing from sight.

We maintained our own pace, reflecting our age and fitness. Often, where the trail made a switchback, you had to be extremely careful as it was very easy to go past the turn and find yourself on the mountain, separated from the trail and having to create your own way.

We soon found ourselves higher and higher up the mountain. The valley stretched out below us with the thin straight ribbon that delineated the course of the asphalt river with a constant flow of lorries, buses and cars.

Many times, I had looked up from there.

Now, part way to my goal, I was gazing down.

We rested. We photographed the sea of wild flowers until it became apparent we had enough pictures of the blue ones, and the red ones, and the white ones.

Then we stumbled on something totally unexpected. We were halfway up a mountain. It was hot and there was no water. And what did we see? There were **large turtles** on the slope.

'What are they doing up here, halfway to the top of the mountain?' I asked no one in particular.

They were large. Yes, 'they' as we saw three. They were probably 20 to 25 cm in diameter, although they were more oval than round.

We often found the going hard. There were large rocks, sheer rocks, and such to navigate around. The slope was steep and there were bracken and tough mountain bushes everywhere.

'How do these turtles make their way?' I wondered.

'Where do they get water?'

The questions came, but no answers. It suffices to say they were there, up the mountain and on the move.

We were two thirds of the way up the mountain when I saw a subgroup of the young people making the climb. We were on the trail - this I knew. They were once ahead of us, but now they were below us.

One of us, or so it looked to me, was off the trail. In the end, it appeared they had missed a switchback and were making their own way in the brush, boulders and other impediments on the mountainside. They joined up with us for the final stretch.

Finally, just an hour after we began, we crested the side of the hill and there was the castle, serene and calm, sitting on a peak with the valley falling away on three sides.

A great view – and the realisation of a long held desire. I was at, even in, Keçi Kale. 'Whoopee!!'

There below us we could see down the one valley to Selçuk and then in front of us up the other valley where the road to Alaşehir [1](ancient Philadelphia) would have been. We also saw a great expanse of the plain still flooded from the unusual amount of rain this year. Finally, up the valley to the left, was the road going to Izmir.

*From Keçi Kale looking down*

For years I had looked 'up'. *Now I was looking 'down'*. A satisfied grin graced my face from ear to ear.

After a rest, a look around and some photos, we began the descent. We had followed the trail up, but now the group headed down the 'direct route' – *sans* trail. This was not an 'official' decision. But they took off as one, intent on descending by the shortest possible route in the shortest possible time.

We were dead last and trying vainly to keep up. We were not old but, compared to the rest, we were.

No trail – we were charged to make our own. We found it steep; it was very steep, sometimes too steep. But we carefully negotiated each challenge and pressed onwards.

Peer pressure finds you in unusual places. The young people would not leave us on the mountain. They would be there when we arrived at the bottom. But we, or more pointedly, I, was always feeling the need to go faster. We are dead last and getting laster.

Tülin was not enjoying this plunge over the mountainside. So when we stumbled on the trail, I thought it best to abandon the overland route and to follow the trail the rest of the way down. We had about halfway to go. It would be more enjoyable and imminently more do-able. After all, it wasn't a race.

And so we went – still pushing the pace, trying not to keep the others waiting longer than we had to.

They were innocent — they had said nothing to us. This was my fault. I was not wanting to keep others waiting for me. We followed the trail. There were switchbacks and in places a regular trail. In other places half a trail and we had times of 'well, there is a trail around here somewhere'.

We were on a half-trail spot. I was in front when I heard the sound that you never want to hear. Tülin had put her foot down as you do when you are walking. Now, whether it was a slippery stone, a rock moved, or… well we don't know what, her foot went out and down she came. It was one of those unintended, undesired and uncon-trolled events that often decorate our lives.

Not a pretty sound.

Not a happy activity for Tülin. I turned and there she was, kind of sitting on the trail with her left leg out in front.

Her face reflecting her feelings. 'Pull my foot,' she said.

I thought, 'What do I know about bones out of joint, or broken bones or things like that, I don't know what to do.'

Her tone shifted as she repeated, 'Pull… My… Foot!!' — note the double exclamation marks. Sometimes you do as requested without worrying about the niceties like 'what am I doing'.

Well, her ankle appears to be NOT broken. Good. But whatever it is, it is NOT normal. There is no question of it being NOT affected. It wasn't the worst-case scenario, but it wasn't good either. It was bad.

Twisted, injured, bruised — not sure what exactly.

She could, um…well… 'walk' would be the *wrong* word. I think 'hobble' would describe it best. So I took the things that she had been carrying and we headed off on the remaining segment of our descent. There was no rushing this process.

'Ooo — ow', 'Ooo — ow'; two different sounds, two different pains. She hobbled on as we slowly worked our way down the trail. The time for overland jaunts had passed. It was difficult going. Walking or hobbling, you put pressure on your ankle.

The surface was varied, sometimes smooth, sometimes steep. In places it was strewn with stones and sometimes with stones hidden in the grass. But step by step, little by little, the trip was completed and we arrived back at the van.

We set out to conquer the mountain and attain the castle. We were brought low by a wee stone. Things do not go as we plan or desire.

What to say? We do our best, and deal with the rest.

# 8

# June 2003 - Flight or Fight?
## - This Day, No Question

I could feel the tension in the air as I stood stock-still, eyes alert, my pupils darting back and forth. I was fully in a 'flight or fight' adrenaline rush. But today there would be no flight, it was to be a fight.

I pivoted my body slowly to the right and spied my prey. Ah, a clever girl she was too, resting so confidently on the ceiling. She was well out of reach of the biped on the floor. Little did she appreciate the resourcefulness of this biped.

I flicked the towel. This was a skill learned in my youth and used with indiscriminate abandon in pursuing childish pleasure. The towel flew with the speed of a meteor upward towards the ceiling. Mind you, it was not very accurate, but it travelled with substantial force. The object of my fury, sensing danger, immediately took flight. However, the air disturbance caused by the towel meant that a miss was as good as a hit.

The resultant pass of the towel disrupted the air. She lost control and spiralled helplessly out of control, finally coming to a halt on the bathroom floor. Dazed but uninjured, there was still flight left in her wings. But that ended when my foot came crashing down. It completed the job and brought to an end to the reign of terror caused by the little madam. One less mosquito terrorising the world.

OK, you might think I'm taking it personally. But when they descend on you, buzzing in your ear, disturbing your peace and rest – well, it does become personal.

Amazingly, small things can have a disproportionate effect on us.

How bad can a wee mosquito be? After all, it is so small and we are so big. Just one is enough to disturb your peace. One, if it is carrying malaria, suffices to give you the disease. It's easy to belittle the little things, but little things can be important and often are important.

Malaria is in Turkey, but it is not widespread. However, the threat is real. It was time well spent dealing with the little madam.

# 9

# August 2003 - A Baptism in the English Channel

I n 2002 we moved from the UK to Turkey. And a year later we moved from Selçuk to İstanbul. We were trying to develop a new work. But we were still connected to our old life in the UK. For eleven years we had built friendships and worked with people in a small Christian work in London. That work continued - it was not 'our' work after all, but God's.

However, in August 2003, we were once again in England.

I was apprehensive as I drove down the narrow lane towards the sea. I laboured to keep to my side of the road on a road that wasn't of sufficient width to support more than one side. As I reached the end, there were cars parked in every available place. I found a spot that wasn't a spot, but I thought it would do. I left the car and clambered up the steep man-made bank. This bank was built to keep the English Channel at bay during winter storms.

The view on the opposite side would have been humorous if you were expecting the sea to be lapping at the brink of the dike. The water was down, way down. And it was out, way out. The tide was at its lowest. We had gathered for a baptism in the sea. But if we were to have the baptism at that hour, we would all have to work our way down a rather steep shingle bank. And once there, we would have a lengthy, leisurely stroll across the mud flats to where the waves were breaking in the distance.

Thankfully, the baptism was not scheduled for several hours and the tide was turning. Would it be enough? Would the water arrive at the dike so we could have the baptism without a half mile trek across the shingle, sand and mud?

I returned to the site of this year's annual Çare[1] Family Camp for Turkish-speaking folk living in London. This was the first year that we had not been intimately involved in every aspect of planning and running the camp. When I arrived at the camp, the new leader, Seido, was at the entrance to the camp. He asked, 'Would you help and run a chap down to the train station in Hastings?'

'Of course', I said. And off I went, glad to be of service.

On my return, I checked the sea again. The tide was on its way in… But would it arrive on time? After the morning meeting, I again took a stroll to the sea to find the welcome sight of the sea racing in. The baptism would be with the sea near and deep. The previous year we had multiple baptisms and the tide was out (and going out). Everyone hiked out to the shallows for the event. But it would be nice this year, with the tide in and everyone able to take part without the clamber and hike.

And this year, of the half-dozen people who are discussing baptism, only one was ready. It was an extreme blessing and honour to witness this lady follow the Lord in the waters of baptism. We gathered on the shingle beach, sang worship to our Lord, and prayed. Then everyone gathered on the sea shore for the baptism. Many English people were avidly watching the events unfold before them. Mind you, as a Turkish group, everything, songs and prayers, were in Turkish.

For this event I had a good video camera and monopod. Tülin was holding the mike, complete with a 'squirrel'. (A squirrel is a fuzzy wind noise-blocking thingy.) The person who was baptised was eager to see the video (being baptised, she didn't 'see' it live herself).

*Baptism in the English Channel*

So, I reluctantly agreed to an impromptu showing before we had to leave to return to Hemel[2]. I was reluctant as I had not seen nor heard the footage myself. I hooked everything up, but couldn't get the sound to work. Hmm, maybe a defect in the borrowed kit at the camp. The picture was punctuated with square blocks. Sometimes this, uh, 'effect' was just down the left side. But at other times, it would dominate (and ruin) the whole picture. No sound and blocking picture, not looking good. We tried to play the tape in another camera - same result. It seems the tape from start to finish was no good.

You hold the camera and frame the shot as best you can. You make efforts to capture good sound, even in a breeze.

But technical things are technical things, and all the footage we captured on that tape was no good. The tape shot before this one and the tape shot after were good. Also lost on the tape were interviews with several Turkish people.

We acknowledge the Lord as Lord, even when things do not go as we planned or hoped.

Although the fig tree shall not blossom, neither shall fruit be in the vine . . . yet I will rejoice in the LORD, I joy in the God of my salvation.

Habakkuk 3:17,18 NIVUK

# 10

# October 2003 - When You Have a Need

I am not really sure of the directions. I've not done this before. I have entered the maze that makes up one of the city bus stations down near the Bosphorus. There are city buses and private buses, names of locations - many of which I do not know where they are - and numbers of routes. I am looking for '14Y'. There are many 14s. Finally, I find 'my' bus. On entering I press my '*Akbil*' - this is kind of like a key fob, but the electronic head has been charged with some money and on every use the fare is deducted from the total. Press the key fob, 'Bee-boop', and I'm on - what a wonderful system!

As I sit waiting for the bus to leave, I ponder the fact that I rushed to find the bus. I dread being in the position where I have missed it by a minute. Now, I am early, and I have eaten nothing for lunch. I haven't even brought a bottle of water. I am on and have paid and hence, I am not about to leave the bus to find water.

Then a simple man enters the bus - and he doesn't pay. His dress is village dress — baggy trousers and shirt. His face is in the perpetual state of not clean-shaven and yet not bearded. He has a blue pail in his hand and in the pail, bottled water. He is a water seller. And he isn't somewhere waiting for me to go to him. No, no, he is out looking for custom. He is searching wherever it may be. Not waiting for people to go to him, his service is to go wherever you are.

I am sitting in our flat in Idealtepe. Idealtepe is on the Asian side of Istanbul, on the banks of the Sea of Marmara. Our flat in Idealtepe is our temporary accommodation. We have left Selçuk and we have not yet purchased a flat in Istanbul. Idealtepe is a typical part of the endless streets and apartment buildings that are Istanbul. It is a new area which has been built in the last 100 years. The old areas of the city are a long way away. Old Istanbul had no concept of automobiles. But in this new Istanbul the roads are wide enough for cars. But over the years city planners lacked the notion that automobiles would become commonplace. Parking is the perennial problem for those who drive in this city.

So, by the time you park vehicles in every legitimate and a few less than kosher places, there is just room for a single track down the road. No passing, basically one way - but officially it is two ways.

One day, sitting there in our flat in Idealtepe, I hear a strange noise outside - some kind of machine. I look out my window and there is a flat bed lorry. On the back is a large table and on one side is a machine. A man and a boy are manhandling a large runner type carpet. They twist and turn it and put it in the machine. As they guide the edge through the machine, two balls of cotton or twine or some material twirl as the thread is pulled off and into the machine. To power all this, they have a small portable power generator. The machine, it seems, finishes edges on carpets.

They finish carpets, but they are also selling carpets. People may come out of their flat, buy a hall runner, get it cut to their length. They then machine finish it on the lorry. They do this right there outside their house. The carpet finisher isn't in a shop waiting for you to come to him; he is out on the streets, looking for you.

You are out and about. And you remember you need something photocopied. Now, you could go to a copy shop and have it done there. Or you could pause on a street corner where a man has a photocopier. He powers this with a small electrical generator. He has them both mounted on a small cart - ready to do your photocopying right there on the street while you wait. If, by any chance, you want it laminated, well, there is another chap standing nearby with a cart, generator and laminator - waiting to serve you.

If you were to spend an hour or two looking out of our living room window, you would see many people passing by: a chap looking for your throw-aways, sellers of vegetables, water, bottled gas, plastics, cleaning supplies, and many other products and services. All brought to your door. Full service, and with a smile.

The Turkish attitude to work is proactive. Yes, you can go to shops, malls, markets and other places to buy various things. But, there is an entire army of people bringing their goods and services to you, wherever you may be.

# 11

# November 2003 - Shopping - Alaturka

A while back, we were expecting a visitor to come and stay with us. As we did not have a place for them to rest their weary head after their travels, we went out in search for a sofa bed.

Upon entering the shop, we began looking at the wares on offer. There were many singles, but I felt that too limiting and was looking for something that would make out to a double bed. We went downstairs in the shop to a room filled wall-to-wall with sofa beds. Of course you want to see not just the sofa bit, but the opened-up bit as well – and that requires space. But in that large room there was no open space.

No problem. A couple of people are called, the owner comes to supervise and sofas are shifted and moved to make room.

If I inadvertently glanced at one, immediately a chain of events was started so that one was freed from the bondage of the tight columns of sofas lined up in the room. I had said nothing, but they had made it ready if we might want to see it opened up as well.

For me, this engendered mixed emotions.

With one furtive glance, I knew I had no interest in that sofa. But, because of the minor glance, it was freed. They were labouring in the hope of a sale and 'in the event' that we may wish to see this sofa. I had great power. A mere glance at a sofa and immediately people sprang into action. They were busy shifting, lifting, lugging and otherwise doing everything necessary that the sofa may be set free. Their goal was to bring it into a space where we may see it in all its glory, closed and open.

All this without saying a word.

After examining the wares, the dickering on price began. I am hopeless in the Turkish art of price negotiations. Hopeless. In the end, we agreed a price.

Like I said, I'm not good at bartering, but it was a price that I felt was appropriate for the goods and which I was happy to pay.

Upstairs we go. There we sat down with the owner.

'I don't have the money with me,' I said.

'No problem,' he replied. 'When you have it, come by – it's not important. Give me your address and I can have the sofa bed delivered immediately.'

And then tea was ordered. We drank, we chatted, we finished. Then we rose. We hadn't paid a penny. We made no down payment. In fact, we hadn't signed a paper. We left.

The sofa bed was duly delivered half an hour later.

Oh, remembering the scriptural admonition to 'owe no man anything but the debt of love'[1] I went two days later and paid the bill.

He was surprised and said there was no hurry. Ah, doing business in Turkey is not like I have experienced in the West.

# 12

# November 2003 - My Eyes Focused Slowly

He stretched his hand out towards me. The chap was speaking, and I was hearing him, but I wasn't really listening. My attention was drawn to his outstretched hand and the object he was giving me.

'This was not what we had agreed,' was my **only** thought. It kept repeating in my mind like an endless video loop. I tuned in to what he was saying, 'You go right out of this building, to the first street, turn right again, and go down the hill and there it is.'

'So, older brother, that is where the van is,' he finished.

The plan, or my understanding of the plan, was at extreme variance. I thought we had agreed he was going to bring the van, which we were borrowing, over to the Asian side of the city where we live. Then another brother and I would drive to Bursa to meet some believers and do some research.

Bursa is roughly two hours south of Istanbul. It too has ancient roots. And from 1335 to 1363 it was capital to the Ottoman Empire. My travelling companion wanted to research the local textiles made in Bursa. He was investigating this as a business opportunity for local Christians.

I liked that plan as I would not have to drive in old Istanbul. Istanbul is a city with many faces. In the centre is the oldest part, the descendant of the ancient city. Streets are narrow, often changing names without notice after a few hundred metres. Did I say 'narrow' - you cannot overstate how some ancient laneways have maintained their narrowness throughout the millennia.

So, here we were, in that ancient mega city with roads laid down two thousand five hundred years ago. I had not planned to drive in old Istanbul. I was not prepared. I had bought an 'A-Z' street map of the city the day before. But, alas, it was at home.

Of course it was.

I had no plans to drive anywhere when I went to this meeting on the European side of the city. I was not ready. Nor did I have a clue how I would get from where I was to where we live. The last time I drove on that side of the city was back in 1981! And I couldn't remember a lot from then. I was not prepared emotion- ally to take charge of a borrowed van. Nor was I prepared to head into Istanbul's rush-hour traffic. To make matters worse, it was a wet, overcast day, and it was getting dark. All I had to do was feel my way across the city and across the Bosphorus. Then, find the right road that would take me to my area and finally to our flat.

Easy-peasy is **not** how I would describe the task before me.

I asked, 'What is the licence plate of the van?' It had been several years since I had seen the van – maybe he changed it for a new one. 'The number is 34, MB, and *something else*,' he replied.

Ah, that is a big help. All cars in Istanbul city AND Istanbul prov- ince begin with 34. So, if all I have is 34, I am looking for one vehicle among hundreds of thousands, nay millions, in this mega city. The second letters are MB. This is both good and bad. Good because all foreigners cars have 'MB' for the letters. This narrows it some, but it is still fairly general. The last numbers, the ones that would make it all clear – **well, he couldn't remember them.**

So, with fear and trepidation, I took the key from his hand — alas, I had no choice. I smiled a thin smile of acceptance and made my way to the door. I followed his directions and took the turn, and the next turn, and the descent. The search for the van had begun.

Lord help!

'He hasn't bought a new van,' I almost shouted with joy. I recognised the vehicle. Indeed, the licence plate started with 34 MB and *I can't remember the rest.*

Now, how do I go from where I am to where I need to be? It was getting dark. The bridge would be chock-a-block and I did't know how to get to the bridge from where I was. And if I used the bridge, I didn't know how to get to the road that I knew as the E5. I knew the road as E5 - but it had been renamed. Hence, road signs would be of little help - I did not remember the new name.

Then I remembered, 'There is a car ferry near here which goes to the other side.' I asked, got directions, and headed towards the ferry quay. Before long, I found myself in the midst of road construction. I was forced to make turns. I went left, right with a bump up and down. And unexpectedly I came to some lights and I could turn the way I wanted to!

I'm a happy man.

One more turn and there was the ferry terminal. This was a good thing. But it was on the opposite side of the road. And there was a massive concrete barrier designed specifically to keep me from my desired destination. I drove past the ferry terminal, going absolutely the wrong way. This was not good. Nor was there any place to stop or turn – just onwards…

After a while, there was a place to turn around and soon I found myself heading back towards the terminal. This time, however, I was on the correct side of the road. I drove into the terminal. After buying my ticket, I drove in to the waiting area and parked up. I was waiting for the next ferry.

The ferry arrived and disgorged its cargo of vehicles and people. We then drove on board and after a bit, our voyage began.

'Ah, this is the way to cross the Bosphorus,' I thought, sitting at the steering wheel. We sailed sublimely across the dark waters of this international waterway, the ferry gently rolling with the waves. There were ferries to the right, ferries to the left, and ocean-going ships ploughing through the middle.

For me, there was no stress, no strain and what a view.

Fantastic.

We arrived and all were frenetically piling off the ferry. 'But where am I?' was the thought swimming through my mind. I turned right – well, I knew that left was wrong. I travelled down a road and through some more construction. The road then morphed into a four-lane road. And this was the road once identified as the E5.

Wonderful.

In my heart, there was a truly heartfelt prayer of thanksgiving. 'Thank you Lord.' I was on the road that I knew, albeit twenty-odd years ago.

Down the E5, I turned at the turning for the area of town known as Bostancı[1]. Down to the right, past the Luna Park[2], I took a left. I carried on until I saw a pedestrian overpass; I recognised it. There I took a right, passed the mosque, followed by another right and an immediate left and I was home!

Another heartfelt, '***Praise the Lord.***'

I did not want to do this. I wasn't excited about it. I didn't know the way. And yet it had to be done. By God's grace, it was done.

There are many, many things in life that are new, that don't go according to 'plan'. Often we don't know the way forward, sometimes feeling intimidated, sometimes apprehensive. New things that must be done, things we may not feel prepared for.

We step out in faith, not knowing the way, and yet trusting our Sovereign God will show the way and bring us safely to our destination. We press on.

# 13

# November 2003 - The Lifeblood of Istanbul

I stood on our terrace, gazing over the expanse of the Bosphorus Strait. I have read the original name was 'ox ford'. This is hard for me to get my mind around. I mean, it is 30 kilometres long linking the Black Sea with the Marmara Sea. At its widest the strait is 3.7 kilometres, but near the mouth, where it joins the Black Sea, it is only 750 metres wide. That seems like a long way to swim oxen. It seems like a very long way considering the strong currents.

The sun sparkled brightly off the dancing blue waters. The sharp prow of the sleek white passenger ferry sliced through the waters. Sunbeams brightly sparkled in the spray as it flew away from the prow.

This was one of six ferries within my field of vision. Each one was moving back, forth, up and down the crowded waterway. And each one had its own route; where it came from and where it is going. Each ferry was laden with its human cargo.

*The ships... the ships...*

Mixed with these large passenger ferries, there were two car ferries plying the strait. These car ferries were loaded with cars and lorries of all descriptions. They ponderously trudged across the strait. They are designed with two fronts and no back. This is to make it easy to load and unload their mobile cargo.

But there was more, much more. Where there are fish, you have fishermen. And as the Bosphorus is a major fish migration route, there was a large school of fishing boats. Before me there were many small, one-man boats; some of them no bigger, it seemed, than a rowing boat.

I was stunned by the movement of the ferries, human and car, and the dozens of these little fishing boats. The fishing boats were solely intent on the business of catching fish. They were slow moving and oblivious to everything happening around them. The ferries plied around and often through their midst.

To this, we added passenger motor-ferries. These are smaller than the larger ferries. To describe them, the locals refer to them as 'motors'. The large state-run ferries carry hundreds of people per journey. But the smaller motor-ferries carry up to a hundred and fifty. Their routes ply between the opposing sides of the Bosphorus; knitting the two halves of the city together. They are slower than the larger ferries and there are far more of them. They twist, turn, and plough forth on their assigned course.

Guess what? We were not done yet.

Then there were the high-speed ferries. They are twin hulled hydrofoils. They are like a cross between an airplane and a ferry.

They are fast, very fast, manoeuvring amongst the ferries, car and human, fishing boats and motors. The spray they generate rises like twin rooster tails from behind their sterns. Their mission is to be the fastest ferry on the water.

There was one more.

Finally, we added the spectacle of ocean-going ships making their way either up or down in the middle of the passage. Some ride high, showing they are going to collect their goods. While others sit low in the water because they are fully laden. Every cargo leaving or going to the Black Sea has only this strait to use. So, from the benign to the dangerous, all traverse this narrow strait.

Ships are designed for the open sea. It is unnatural for them to be hemmed in by the narrow course of the strait. And to make it more challenging, it is not straight nor of a uniform width. Their natural home is the open sea, not the narrow twisting confines of the strait. And they face a multitude of ferries crossing in front and behind them. Sometimes it looks like the ferries are aimed directly at immense freighters.

It may not look like it, but this is a controlled waterway. Well, the fishing boats seem to be exempt. The ferries bide their time, waiting for the intruding hulks to pass out of the way. Sometimes I thought there was ample room - but the ferry was ordered to wait.

It is a sight that takes my breath away. I stand, mesmerised by the dance of the various elements. Each is intent on their own business and yet each taking its place amongst the whole. This happens in the waters of the Bosphorus every day. It is always the same, and yet never the same.

It is vibrant and changing. They are knowing and not knowing, all being a part of something and being estranged from it at the same time. Every day this dance is played out. The vessels are teaming with life – well, with tens of thousands of passengers per day. They are not tied to the ship – but a mere passing commodity.

Life — our lives and actions reflect this in a thousand ways every day. We live on this lump of dirt flying through space but not alone. Knowing this, we are aware of the fact that we are travelling together and not together. We are not all going to the same destination. We have many traits and things in common with the surrounding multitude, and yet we are unique. Each one is one of a kind and we are on our own journey.

But we are not travelling alone. We are in a sea of fellow travellers. Each of us going our own way - trying not to collide with any other.

# 14

# January 2004 - What Good is a Wee Light?

I crack open the window and feel the immediate force of the cold wind as it attempts to force the window fully open. I lean forward, straining to see through the slats of the shutters. I can just make out ghostly white images. All is indistinct and clouded as the snow hides all light. It is an overpowering darkness that the fresh blanket of snow brings. There is no movement other than that caused by the violent gusts of wind. No light shines, just a pervading darkness in every direction. It is after sunset; it is snowing, and the electricity supply has failed.

When we lived in Turkey in the early 1980s, the cutting of electricity was done by the clock. The electricity board would move the supply from neighbourhood to neighbourhood. I remember being in someone's home as the clock drew nigh to 20:00. I knew, and it wasn't my house, but even I knew the power would go off at 20:00. No one moved, no preparations were made. And, at the stroke of 20:00, all was plunged into darkness.

But tonight, in 2004, the cutting of the electricity is not driven by an inadequate supply. It is more a reaction to unexpected load or weather interference. Things get wet, or knocked over in the wind, and the power goes. It is unpredictable - except when the weather turns stormy; you prepare for the power to go out.

This is true in all the cities of Turkey and it even extends to the biggest city — Istanbul.

I push the window shut and turn into the pitch darkness of the house, moving carefully towards the stairs. Our home comprises two floors, the main floor with the living room, bathroom, spare bedroom and kitchen. The lower floor with a toilet, bedroom and workroom. As I move towards the stairs, the light of the candle that we have placed in the lower hall shines brightly before me. This small, insignificant candle is making things clear and distinct. Hence, I can tell steps from shadows and I can move forward with greater confidence.

*This little light of mine...*

It is amazing how much light a single candle can give. The tiny flame on top of a slender tube of wax shines and fills the corridor in an amazing abundance of light. This wee light providing safety in negotiating the stairs and the curve at the bottom. It is also bringing cheer and brightening the heart with its glow. We have positioned candles in the hall, toilet and work room; these three small candles create seas of light in the winter darkness.

As is often the case in our modern world, the house slowly chills with the absence of the central heat system. The complex machinery is lying still because of the deficiency of electricity – silent and unstirring. The phone ceases to work and the computer, well the laptop will work for as long as the battery lasts.

There is no danger. We will not freeze to death. Yes, there is snow, but it does not feel that cold and these houses are like modern caves against the elements. This represents minor discomfort but no more.

This small candle beside me, providing me light and comfort and reassurance as I type these few words. It reminds me of something that happened just a few days ago.

Tülin and I had just returned from the UK. We rejoiced in the Lord for the completion of the sale of our house. In 2002, we had made 'the move' from the UK. And yet, with the house in the UK, and us in Turkey, we were still here and there. Our plan was to sell there, to buy here. Buying here naturally depended on selling there.

The plane landed in Istanbul and our journey was nearing an end. We were looking forward to getting 'home'. We took the service bus from the airport to the sea bus terminal. The sea bus, as the name implies, is a ferry service plying routes across the Bosphorus. The actual vessel is a twin-hulled, high-speed ferry. There was quite a walk from where the service bus dropped us and the sea bus. This walk was made more difficult as we made a small, but significant, error.

When travelling, your life is reduced to 23 kilos each. The most important issue seems to be weight. It is an important issue, but it is also important to remember that we have only two hands each. What this means is we should have had only four bags.

We had five.

Now it wouldn't have been too much of a problem but for a new bag — a gift we received in the UK. This was its maiden flight - its first time flying. And on its first outing, all the wheels had been torn off the bag. It was large and heavy. Now, sans wheels, it would have to be carried and not dragged.

By the time we reached the sea bus, I wasn't going to lug the luggage one foot or centimetre further than I had to. So, once on board, we collapsed in the nearest seats. These were at the front of the boat. All the seats in the ferry face forward. All, that is, but one row at the very front which faces the back. This was not my first choice in seating - I prefer to be facing the way we are going. But, as I said, I was not going to move the luggage any further than necessary. All the front facing seats near the door were full, just the awkward ones facing the back were free.

As I sat there, looking towards the back of the boat, before me sat some two or three hundred fellow passengers. Some were reading and others in discussion. There were the obligatory individuals chatting loudly away on their mobile telephones, to the annoyance of all around. Still others were taking this opportunity to catch a few winks of sleep. And others were simply staring into space.

Two or three hundred people just like you and me. They had fathers and mothers, sons and daughters. They worked or went to school. Each one had dreams, fears, problems, struggles, aspirations, encouragements and discouragements. They were just like you and me.

They were people who laugh at funny things and cry at sad things. They were people who wanted to have a full and happy life. And, they were people who faced the same, everyday problems of life that you and I face.

I sat in my seat, surrounded by the luggage. I was catching my breath and feeling new muscles speaking out against the journey so far. But something struck me as my eyes raised and gazed at my fellow travellers. I left my petty complaints and looked at the faces of the people before me. Here were two to three hundred people who had never heard the Good News of an '**abundant life**' or of a '**new life**'. They were completely ignorant of the *offer* to be '**reconciled with God**' and of '**knowing Him**'.

They were doing their best to live their lives. But they had never had a single opportunity to hear and understand all that is in Christ.

This is what our journey is all about. We want to be there, to give these lovely people an opportunity - *if they wish*. They have their dreams and aspirations. They live with their disappointments and discouragements. All we desire is to give them is their first opportunity to hear the Good News.

Currently, it is said, there are somewhere between 1,000 and 3,000 Muslim background believers in the whole country. (This number was accurate when written in 2004. In 2015, the number is considered being between 4,000 and 5,000. The population of the country in 2004 was 67,000,000.)

My little candle makes all the difference in the house. Without it, I would stumble, even though I know the house well. In its absence, I would have difficulty with the basic tasks of life that must be done. Without it, there is very little I could do. And that which I may attempt to do would be difficult and fraught with hidden dangers. My simple little candle makes a fantastic difference in the darkness.

So, we, feeling feeble, unworthy and insufficient to the task, can be a 'wee candle' shining in darkness. Likewise, for you, wherever you are. In whatever situation you find yourself, whether you feel great or small, you can be that 'wee candle' in the darkness you find yourself in.

# 15

# February 2004 - The Light Blue Mist

The light blue mist caused by the cigarette smoke drifted lazily in the air as I focused on the man opposite. He was expounding forcefully on some point that my Turkish had failed to even begin to comprehend. I was in the dark. He was speaking quickly and with purpose. His hands were flying into the air or shooting out at right angles to emphasise or punctuate his harangue.

Our purpose was to haggle about the price of a flat in Istanbul. This was a newly built flat - in an old building.

How do you have a newly built flat in an old building, you wonder? The building was strengthened against earthquakes - and as part of the project, two new flats were built on top. The new flats had matchless views of the Bosphorus Strait.

There, opposite me, two brothers were sitting. These were the men who had strengthened the apartment building. As part of the payment for their work, they had received the two flats added to the top of the building. It is from the sale of these two flats that they would make their profit.

The first price they had put on the flat was an airy-fairy price of near on $250,000 USD. But there were no buyers at that price. But they had bills from the build that they needed to pay. They needed to sell one flat and they needed to sell it soon.

Üsküdâr, where the flat is situated, is a religiously conservative area.

It is situated on the banks of the Bosphorus. Daily ocean-going ships struggle through the narrow strait. And the flat we wanted had an exquisite view of the strait. Added to that, Üsküdâr is near the heart of the old city. It has great connections to, well, everywhere.

These men were religious. They were not 'nominal' but practicing; and the one brother, fully practicing. It was this brother who would not shake my wife's hand. For him, it would be a sin to touch a woman, even to shake her hand. He was a 'hafiz' – a person who has memorised the whole text of the Koran – in Arabic. His mother tongue is Turkish, nevertheless, he has fully memorised the Koran in Arabic. He may or may not understand the text — understanding is not essential; being able to recite it is.

We had an intermediary, a representative, someone whose Turkish was impeccable – uh, he was a Turk. And his knowledge in this area was unequivocal. Formerly, he had been a building contractor. He was here, acting on our behalf. So, although I was a key player in this meeting, it soon became apparent it wasn't important for me to know the details or nuance of the situation.

The discussion was primarily between our emissary and the man opposite me — the hafiz. The other people in the room were following the proceedings with care and interest. From time to time a question was raised. Then the estate agent would pick up his phone and find the answer.

Tülin was sitting opposite and to the right of me, against the wall. Things were definitely looking like they had gone badly pear-shaped. It seemed it was only a matter of time before the debate and verbal sparring would end in abject failure.

We were lost in the finer points of the language. But the gesturing and emphatic declarations were clear. The conclusion of the matter seemed near and negative.

Finally, and to our eyes, rather abruptly, our negotiator sprang to his feet. He crossed the room to the man he had been waging single-handed verbal combat with. He reached out and grasped his right hand and with mighty strokes shook his hand as one might pump water from a well.

He then crossed the room to the man's brother. This brother was the other major player in the room and repeated the gesture.

Then he crossed to me, grabbed my right hand. He put my hand in the right hand of the *hafiz*. And with the same exaggerated style he moved our hands up and down in a handshake manner. A lot of water could have been pumped from a well that day.

But it was done!

They had just sold, and we had just bought a flat in Istanbul. Or at least we had agreed to. The process was rather more drawn out and Byzantine in practice. As I am a foreigner, the sale had to be referred to the military.

And when time to pay came, it would have to happen via bank transfer. No longer, or so we were told, did you arrive at the Land Registry office with a bag stuffed full of cash. This was a new legal requirement and a stumbling block to the *hafiz*. Being very devout, he believed it was a sin to have a bank account — usury is expressly forbidden in the Koran. But to be paid, he had to have a bank account to receive the money. The final step was the essential paper-work at the Land Registry Office. But all of that was still in the future. We had agreed to buy the flat. There was still over a month, nearly two, before we could actually call the deal 'done'.

We learned of the flat through our intercessor — he found it. And without him, we would not have been able to agree on the purchase of the flat. He had worked them down from their asking price to their 'final' price and then below that. He had them agree to be responsible for any fines that may have been incurred in the construction — and there were some. He also had them agree to installing radiators.

But we did not have enough money to buy the flat. Some dear friends — tired of paying rent — agreed to a shared ownership scheme with us. They would buy a 13% share. The flat was a large two floor affair. The lower floor was a proper flat and the upper floor a wee granny flat. We agreed to share the property - a truly shared ownership situation. And this made the deal possible. Our emissary negotiated, cajoled, encouraged and, understanding the culture and the process, brought the deal to completion. Our friends brought the needed funds to the table to complete the deal. We couldn't have done it without the Lord's provision of these two parties.

Our move to Turkey, and our purchase of this flat with the amazing view, was made possible by God. He provided the funds from the sale of our home in England. And He provided a local emissary. As a former builder, he counselled on the suitability and engineering qualities of all the flats we looked at. And he understood the bureaucracy and what needed to be done. Being a Turk, he was able to negotiate the deal properly. Finally, he helped us without charge. Last, but not least, God provided friends who were ready and keen to become part owners with us in this venture.

It is never the story of one person. Life is the story of the 'many' that God brings together to accomplish His purposes. In the above account, my job was to sit and say nothing. Oh, yes, I was called upon to shake hands when the time came. Our friends' job was to come in as part owners. Our helper's job was to advise, counsel, and close the deal.

We each had a part to play....

# 16

# February 2004 - Ooops

The day was lovely. We had travelled from the Asian side of Istanbul to the European side. But, like every day, darkness fell. Weariness washed over me, and a desire rose from deep within. I wanted to be home, tucked up and comfortably resting.

Our eldest son, John, and his fiancée, Laura, were visiting with us. He had graduated from university and was working in the UK.

We had been to old Istanbul.

The city, back in 660 BC was called Byzantium.

Across the Bosphorus was Chalcedon. It was founded before Byzantium. However, it was said those who founded and lived in Chalcedon — directly across from Byzantium — must have been blind. The site of Byzantium was perfect. Surrounded by water on three sides with a sheltered inlet for a harbour. It was and is an ideal location.

Constantine the Great renamed Byzantium in 324 A.D. He did this when he moved the centre of the Roman Empire to this site. No longer was Rome, in the west, to be the capital. Now it was Constantinople, in the centre of the empire. He remodelled the city in stone — hastily — and renamed it after himself. It remained Constantinople until 1453 A.D. It was 29 May in that year that the rump of the Byzantine empire, now consisting mainly of the city, fell to the conquering Turks under the leadership of Sultan Mehmed II. He was titled Mehmed the Conqueror after taking the city. He made the former capital of the Byzantine Empire the new capital of the Ottoman Empire.

Regardless of its name, we had spent the day in old Istanbul. We had finished the day with a tour of the Topkapı palace, the capital of the Ottoman empire for hundreds of years.

One of the gates into the Topkapı[1] palace

The Topkapı palace is typical of royal establishments that exist over long periods of time. It was added to and expanded endlessly. And it was outgrown and in later years the Sultans built new, grander palaces in which to live and govern. One of the last palaces to be built is called 'Dolma Bahçe[2]'.

The Ottomans were painted as the bogeyman by western powers. But they were a great empire which lasted for over 600 years. Unlike the English system of divide and conquer - they let the local peoples live with some freedom. But it was always under the watchful eye of the Sultan.

Despite the western tainted picture — it was a great empire. You can see the fruits of the empire in the Topkapı palace museum.

There are three parts of the museum. There is the residence of the Sultan and his harem. There is the throne room where the work of the empire was conducted. The kitchens that served the seat of power are on display. There is the treasury which will take your breath away with its endless displays of wealth and gold. For me, the most amazing things are two solid gold candlesticks. They are decorated with a diamond for every verse in the Koran. Then there is the portrait collection of the Sultans and the leading men of the Empire. Finally, there is the part of the museum dedicated to the Prophet Muhammed. There is an extremely old copy of the Koran held in the museum and, reportedly, a footprint of the prophet, a sandal, some of his hair, his sword and other artefacts.

That room was packed with the faithful. There were women in a variety of head coverings, men with the small white skullcap, and a multitude of children, all doing a sort of pilgrimage. The parents were showing the artefacts to their children. And the adults were staring at the artefacts that confirmed the historicity of their prophet. In a corner, in a small booth, sat a man in a long dull-coloured robe with a squarish turban on his head. He had a clean, close-cropped beard. His eyes were closed as he sat before an open Koran, rocking gently, chanting verses from memory. This sound filled the room and invaded every recess of the mind.

It had been a good day. With my smaller, but good quality video camera, I had taken some video which I felt was 'good' stock footage. You never know when you may need some footage from Istanbul, the palace or the general environs. As always, the camera bag was slung over my shoulder. And, as always, at the ready for that important impromptu shot. We were tired and slowly trudged back to the ferry terminal. There we would board the ferry for the half-hour ride across the Bosphorus to the Asian side.

As always, there was a crush of people waiting in the departure lounge. Our timing was horrible; rush hour had begun. When the doors opened, it triggered a mad dash to board. We were swept along in the human torrent.

In one sense it is unnecessary to rush. The ferry will take all who wish to board. And there is an abundance of seats. So, probably all passengers will have a seat. In my defence, we wanted seats together. Oh, and me being me, I wanted a certain part of the ferry, hence the rush.

The 'no smoking' winds have blown across Turkey as they have across Europe and North America. Therefore, the interior of the ship is all non-smoking. Those who wish to imbibe must go to the open deck to engage their addiction. We settled nicely on some wooden benches, grateful for the opportunity to rest.

**Normally** the ferry goes straight over to Kadıköy[3]. My plan was that we would walk the ten or fifteen minutes from the Kadıköy ferry terminal back to the main train station at Haydarpaşa[4].

Haydarpaşa has its own ferry quay — but this is used only at certain times of the day — all unknown to me. From this train station we would take the commuter train to where we were staying. All this was before we bought the flat in Üsküdâr.

Suddenly I became aware the ferry was slowing as to stop. We had not arrived at Kadıköy, so I did not know what was happening. I wondered if it was possibly stopping at the train station. It seemed possible to me, but unexpected. To validate what I thought was happening, I leaped up from the bench seat. I left the others wondering what was causing my sudden burst of energy. I moved through the crowd to the middle door to see if we were indeed stopping at Haydarpaşa.

Truly, and happily for us, tired travellers all, we were stopping. The large crowd at the door showed that the regular commuters knew that at this time of the day, the Kadıköy ferry stops at the station. As the ship was nigh on docked and as it probably would not remain long at the quayside, I hurried through the crowd to my party.

'Quick, quick!' I urged the others, 'we are getting off **now**.' Everyone leapt to their feet and in a rushed blur of activity hustled to the departure point. We joined the mass of people crowding at the door. The ferry gracefully sidled up to the quay as if the captain were parking a Volkswagen and not a massive ship several hundred feet long and carrying hundreds of passengers.

Trying to stay together amidst the turmoil, we hurried across the quay. We scampered up the stairs to the famous and historic Haydarpaşa train station. We made our way through the cavernous departure hall and out to the departure platforms.

There was our commuter train and we hastily boarded. Twenty minutes down the line, we collected ourselves and disembarked at the station nearest to where we were staying. As I was climbing the stairs of the underpass in the train station, it struck me.

Something was missing.

Something wasn't right.

What was it?… What was it?…

I stopped in the middle of the stairs and turned. A puzzled expression clouded my face. You know the feeling something is wrong, but you can't put your finger on it.

Then it dawned on me.

I flapped.

I patted my body.

I looked anxiously at my fellow travellers.

Frantically I examined each of my companions; did Tülin have it, did my son, his fiancée?

Alas, no.....

My video camera, the one that went with me wherever I went, had now gone somewhere without me. More likely I had gone some-where without it. Whatever the case, it was most definitely no longer with me.

No more to be said. Did I leave it on the ferry in my haste to depart?

Most likely.

I rang the ferry company. I asked if it had been turned in? I went back the next day to talk with the captain. Nothing was turned in on the ferry itself. It seems someone received an early holiday present. They 'found' an expensive, quality camera, complete with batteries, unused video tape. Not that they would notice, but there was some wonderful stock footage as well.

Regrettably, for me it was gone. And boy, have I missed it. It was so handy. It didn't draw attention in a crowd and yet it recorded very good images. I took it when I travelled and it allowed me to load tape onto the computer for editing on-the-fly.

And it was gone.

It was not a cheap video camera as it cost £1,550 or roughly $3,000 USD, or $3,600 CAD (all 2003 values). It was not something that I felt I was going to replace easily or soon.

Ahh…But God.

I love the passages in the Bible that begin with 'But God'. I did not have the resources to replace this camera. Moreover, I had nothing to sell and no way to raise or earn that kind of money. But God, who can do abundantly more than we can ask or think, provided. We have been able to replace the camera.

Wow! God is Great! And more to the point, **God is *Gracious*!**

Gracious because it was my own haste and lack of attention that resulted in it being left behind. Grace – undeserved, unearned favour.

God is many things: all knowing, all powerful, Creator, Sustainer, Judge, Holy, but maybe the two most powerful attributes of God are His Love and His Grace.

Without these two, where would we be… where would I be?

# 17

# March 2004 - Unseen Forces

*The Mighty Bosphorus*

We stood there transfixed, mouths open. Tülin stopped everything and rummaged around in her bag. 'This,' she thought, 'is a once in a lifetime opportunity.' She found her camera and began taking some quick snaps.

We had seen the view before. But now, standing on our terrace, we gaped at the beauty of the view in front of us. There, stretched out before us, was a large body of water, narrow and long, and teaming with activity. The sleek, fast-moving ferries carrying their load of hundreds of passengers plied their prescribed routes. They were going across and up and down the waterway.

Together they were joined by the privately run ferries plodding about.

Amidst all this, was the high-speed ferry, the sea bus. It flew along, rising part way out of the water on its twin hulls with rooster tails of spray behind each hull.

Dotted here and there were little boats. They moved more like flocks of fishing boats than anything else. These one-man operations were fishing in a group huddle. Wherever they thought there was a school of fish — there they would be.

But all this ignores the elephant in the room. There, ploughing down the centre of the channel, were the big boys. The ocean-going ships of every type, from the massive to the coasters, were represented.

There are two currents in the Bosphorus; one on the surface flowing south and one under the surface flowing north. This makes for challenging eddies and cross currents.

For ocean-going ships, nothing could be more unnatural. Hemmed in on both sides by high hills and being pushed and dragged by unseen currents. They also had to contend with all the local traffic.

*The Dance of Ships - Bosphorus*

This beautiful body of water both joins and divides. It divides the huge city of İstanbul asunder with the west bank in Europe and the east in Asia. All the intercity traffic and trade crosses this body of water.

The water sparkles in the sunshine, but the colour is an amazing deep, inky blue. The surface appears calm. But this is deceptive — there are hidden depths, hidden dangers. There are unseen forces at work, for although it looks placid on the surface – it is not as it first appears.

My eyes were drawn to a ferry on the Üsküdâr–Beşiktaş[1] run. As these two parts of Istanbul are opposite one another, it is a direct route across. As always, the shortest distance between two points is a straight line. So, I expected the ferry to turn and plough straight across.

When the boat starts off, it is pointed straight at Beşiktaş across the strait; the engine, giving its all to cross in the shortest possible time. And yet, although the ferry is aimed directly across the strait, it drifts down towards my left. By the time it has reached the opposite shore, it points up the strait, struggling to make up for lost ground.

They ferry attains his goal, although not according to his intended plan. There are no straight lines when you try to cross this body of water.

Over the past month, I have felt a bit like the ferry. I see where I am going; I am pointed in the right direction. I am doing all in my power to reach my goal and yet I seem to drift sideways, driven by unseen forces.

We found a flat we very much liked. Then we couldn't afford the flat, but a way was found to afford it.

However, before we changed our money from pounds Sterling to Turkish lira, the exchange rate dropped. We no longer had sufficient funds to purchase the flat. And then the rate rebounded, briefly – very briefly. At that precise moment, we exchanged our funds. (Then the rate dropped and remained down for the best part of *ten years*.)

We 'bought' the flat. The torturous process lasted well over a month after we agreed to the sale. We had problems gaining the required military approval. And then that was sorted.

Then, before we could complete, the seller was taken ill. We found out he was not actually ill at all. He had repented of selling the flat for our agreed price and was trying to get out of the deal. And then he relented.

Then I needed to get a residence permit to hook up the utilities. And that was delayed — then sorted.

Finally, the flat was purchased.

Like the ferry, we had arrived. But there was slippage. We were constantly contending with unseen forces.

I turned my eyes back to the Bosphorus. My attention was drawn to the flock of fishing boats. They seem to be stationary in the water. The fishermen were standing, pulling lines or fiddling with some fishing tackle. All the while their little boats were amid all the traffic.

'How…' I asked myself, 'How is it possible for them to be stationary? The much larger ferries are being drawn irresistibly down to the left.' I was flummoxed and muttered to myself, 'How can these little boats remain in the same position?'

And then I saw.

The school of fishing boats was powering upstream. At the same time, there was a constant downstream current. Their upstream speed was an exact match to the rate of the downstream current. This was how they remained in the same place.

Just to be in one place, they must travel forward. To be still, they must move. To do their job, they have to adapt to the challenge and overcome the problem. It looked like the most natural of things.

We all face hidden forces affecting our lives. Our dreams and desires do not go as we hoped. These are reminiscent of these underwater challenges. There are currents and unseen forces affecting our lives. We, by God's grace, find ways of dealing with and overcoming them.

The fishermen have found a way to overcome their circumstance. For us, God provides solutions to the things that inhibit us and we get on with the job.

# 18

# March 2004 - What Could Go Wrong?

I t has been a somewhat hectic time for us. After the sale of our home in the UK, we found a flat to buy in Istanbul.

We were moving into an older building, but into a 'new build' flat at the top. It had never been lived in. And it wasn't fully ready.

But we moved into our new flat as is and then set about getting everything outstanding taken care of.

Our new home has natural gas. But, as our flat is a new build, all we had was a capped-off pipe at the door. It was our responsibility to arrange a gas meter. Oh, yes, and to have a gas fitter come and run the pipes inside the flat. The seller, that is the builder, arranged for 'his man' to come and do the work. We would be only using natural gas for cooking - the heating comes from a central system.

The chap fitting the pipes was diligently working away and was making great progress. His plan looked good. He finished fitting the pipes to the main floor of our flat. Then he began fitting the gas line upstairs. We have a small kitchenette there.

To hold the pipe in place, he was fitting brackets to the walls. In the stairway, he was merrily drilling a hole in the wall when a stream of water burst out.

This was unexpected. A geyser spewing forth out of the wall. Seeing this, I ran downstairs to the stopcocks and turned off the water. However, on my return I found the flow undiminished.

Not to be deterred, I opened a tap in the kitchen to relieve the pressure. But, alas, the water continued to cascade down from the upper level. It flew out a great distance, but gravity, being the greater power, brought it down to the stairs and to the lower level.

What to do? The flow continued, so we put a bucket under it. I rang the builder. I reasoned as he built the place, he would know where the water was coming from.

If we knew what pipe had been pierced, we would know how to stem the flow.

It turned out the pipe serviced the central heating system. Evidently there was a storage tank or some such thing in the loft. All the ruckus and noise drew the building manager. Without so much as a whisper, he turned and left. He descended to the basement where the central heating boiler was. There he simply turned off all the central heat — for the entire building. In its time, and slowly at first, the flow of water stopped.

The pipe fitter, the builder and the building manager discussed how they might fix this hole. It was right at ceiling height and in the stairway. It was in the most awkward of spots. But before it could be repaired, they would need to bust the wall open to see the pipe.

After they drained down our heating system, they let our newly created hole dry out. Then, to plug the hole in the pipe, they used a German epoxy compound. They mixed the two components together which, when dry, form a hard, resilient new compound. This, while still pliable, they put in the hole. The instructions said we would need to wait for three hours. In the end, we waited for the better part of twenty-four. That is a long time with no heat upstairs, let me tell you. Oh, and not just upstairs - it is a central system - the whole building was without heat.

*The fateful location - behind the round plastic cover*
*hiding behind the pipe*

Anyway, when the water was put back on and the central heating system pressurised, the plug held. Rather than bury the repaired pipe, they put an access cap over it. In this way, if the patch were to, uh, unpatch, in the future, at least we won't have to break open the wall again.

# 19

# June 2004 - All Things Looking Mighty Fine

'Swiiiish, swiiish,' the sandpaper sang as I brought my arm down and across the wall in a wide sweeping motion. The air was littered with fine white particles dancing in the light and drifting lazily towards the floor.

With each stroke of my arm, another cloud of fine white dust was released to join the previous stroke in its relentless pursuit of a resting place. The wall was looking fine, very fine indeed.

I was pleased. I stopped sanding. The empty coffee jar that was my make-shift sanding block was not the most efficient, but it was doing the job. I readjusted the sandpaper I had wrapped around the jar and ran my fingers over the wall. Yes, it was feeling fine.

I thought I would soon be finished and then after a quick coat or two of paint, the job would be in the bag. It would be done, completed, finished, out-of-the-way, finito.

Once the wall was done, then the 'storeroom' would be completed and I could finally organise my space and get down to the 'real' work.

I don't know why I did it. I certainly didn't feel the need to do it. There was more than sufficient light and I could see clearly. Indeed, the wall looked good and the drifting mist of plaster dust was certainly visible in the air. After working for a bit and being quite pleased with the results, I flipped the switch, turning on the light.

And then...

And there in the abundance of light, a multitude of flaws, lumps, bumps, lines and a myriad of other defects exploded into sight. A sigh slipped from my lips. This job was going to take more time than I had thought and initially believed.

Tightening the sandpaper wrapped around my coffee jar, I again tackled the wall with a new-found sense of purpose. I would sand, and fill, and sand again, and, when truly prepared, paint this wall, and, yes, 'tick', it would be done. It would be done but not as soon as I had hoped. A set back, certainly, but nothing major; more an inconvenience and yet it had its impact on the task.

This is life. Nothing, so it seems, ever goes to plan. This is important to note. When I undertake a task, I need to allow for the unseen. Too often in life, there are stumbles. The unexpected is, well, 'unexpected'. Things that are firm, when stressed, meet their breaking point. Things that are flexible last longer. Hence, in the tasks of life, I need to adjust and cope with what happens. Because, in life, well, life happens.

# 20

# June 2004 - To Queue or not to Queue - There is no Question

The morning dawned grey and wet. Tülin and I left our flat in Üsküdar, on the Asian side of Istanbul. We headed out for the ferry to cross to Eminönü[1] on the European side. From thence we proceeded on the tramway up to Yusuf Paşa[2]. From the tramway stop, we walked some 400 metres across to the Metro station — part of the Istanbul Underground system. Then it was but one stop up to Emniyet[3]. At this stop is the main police station in İstanbul.

Today was the day we went to *apply* for Tülin's residence permit.

As I had done the process back in March, we had a rough idea of how to go about it. Well, a very rough idea. We went to what I believed was the starting place, only to be told to go to another desk.

We went there. But no one was there and so we waited.

The police officer finally came and told us to fill in a form and have a *dilekçe*[4] — ah, that is an official request — written. Then we were to come back to him.

And so off we went, down a floor, and queued up. There was a man whose job was to write *dilekçes* all day long. On our turn he wrote a standard *dilekçe* and he filled in the form for us. Back we trudged to the desk. But the officer who should be at the desk wasn't there — again.

After waiting a bit, we went off to where we on our arrival had tried to begin. This time an official took the forms and looked things over. He spotted something missing. We needed a photocopy of a page from Tülin's passport. So off I ran to do that. Of course, that was done on another floor.

On my return, the man was content and he sent us to the next desk – the archive. At the door to the archive, we joined the queue. This is a building full of queues. When our turn came, the chap took our details and went off to find Tülin's record. He was searching for her residence permit number from the 1980s.

But he couldn't find it.

He looked under 'D' for her English first name and 'M' for her English surname – in that order. Still no joy. Finally, he sent us off to another office to search for her electronic record.

In this office the man went to the computer and found a record for her – complete with her nickname 'Tülin'. And he found my record, complete with my nickname 'Oğuz' and 'Yenidoğan', for my assumed Turkish surname.

He found all that but no record of her residence permit.

This was puzzling.

So, we returned to the first archive room. There the chap accepted they couldn't find the number and entered her details on the computer and sent us to the next desk.

Naturally, in a building of queues, there we joined another queue.

Now this was a confused queue. It was one queue, but people were actually queuing for two different windows. I like orderly things. I like systems - especially systems that I understand. But what do I do if the person in front of me, is queuing for a different window than me? When was it right to 'jump the queue' — but not really, as they are not going to my window — and when to wait? This was, for me, a painful dilemma.

Finally, we progressed to the head of the queue. The officer on the other side was busy with something, so we waited. When he was ready, he took our papers and asked where Tülin's former residence permit number was?

'Couldn't be found,' replied I.

'Not good enough,' he muttered. Then he added, 'I'll go look in the basement.' *And off he went.*

I don't think we were the most popular people there as my queue watched the man get up and leave the room.

He came back from the basement having found my file (it didn't take him long either). He said we had lovely children — obviously he had looked at the file, that is why he went. He also declared that back then we were all on one residence permit number - and hence they couldn't find a separate number for her.

That explained that.

So, having determined this, he was happy to carry on with his work.

As he processed the paperwork, it was discovered that I needed to photocopy some pages from my residence permit. Oh, yes, AND it was also time to pay for her visa.

So, once again, off we went. Tülin went to an ATM to get some cash. I went to get some photocopies. Then, reunited again, we queued up and paid the fee. It was 680,000,000 TL – yes, in those days it cost us six hundred and eighty *million* Turkish lira! In other money, that was about £2,500 - a lot of money then - and a lot of money now.

This was the one and only time in our lives that we were millionaires — multimillionaires at that.

This done, we returned to the last man we had seen because he needed the photocopy. On our arrival - the queue was still, well, queuing. Our official was busy.

So we waited.

When he was finished with the applicant before him, he waved us forward — we were a work in progress. He took the papers and completed his work. Then he sent us to another window to pay for the residence permit booklet.

Off we went and queued — of course. In the fullness of time, we paid for that, and then joined yet another queue. Now was the time to get it all recorded in the registry — an enormous book.

So we waited in this queue.

When we arrived at the head of that queue, we handed in our papers. He laboriously filled in the massive registry book and gave us a slip. This inconsequential wee slip informed us we must return in three working days to pick up the residence permit.

All in all it was a full, tiring and in some ways demanding day. It was marked with a lot of waiting. There was a lot of fixing things that were wrong, like missing photocopies, dates on documents, spelling of names. We spent a lot of time being in crowded corridors. And we stood a lot and queued a lot.

This was not my idea of an ideal or pleasant day – but it had to be done.

It is days like these that I appreciate the 'Fruit of the Spirit of God' which include long suffering, patience, endurance, love, joy and, maybe most important of all, peace.

It is in the practical activities of life, such as this, that our Faith, our New Life in Christ, have an opportunity to shine and be light and be salt in this world.

The Fruit of the Spirit enables this to be a good day.

# 21

# August 2004 - Reflections in the Water

I settled on the wooden bench on the side of the ferryboat, feeling 'bone weary', as many of us do at the end of a busy day. Given the late hour, I was surprised by the steady stream of people boarding the ferry. They were mostly men worn out from their long day of toil.

The ferry lay at the quayside for about ten minutes. It felt like the ferry, too, was drained by its repetitive toil as it trudged back and forth, a never-ending journey across the Bosphorus Strait. The ferries plied their courses from early morning, through the heat of the day, and into the late evening.

You know when it is getting near time to leave when the dock workers shut all but one door from the terminal. There the man stands, ready to seal it shut, and once shut, no more can board that sailing. And yet he hesitates, with grace, watching for those running to board the ferry. He waits patiently during their mad dash through the turnstile, across the waiting room and out through the last narrow gap. He honours their mustering up one last burst of energy after an arduous day.

The whistle sounds and, with the last doors slammed shut, no more people will board this ferry. Then the crew move to release the mooring lines. The ferry begins with a deep shudder, for it is no longer bound to the quay. There it was in an unnatural and restricted situation. But now, it has come alive. It thrashes the water, as if in a hurry to distance itself from being restrained. The pilot turns this large vessel and it surges into the inky black waters of the strait.

Sitting as I was on the outside, I leaned against the side of the ferry. I felt its throbbing with unseen power and as we moved into the dark waters, my eyes were drawn away from the skyline of this ancient city. I gazed at the reflection of the lights in the flat and docile waters. As night differs from day, so too are the reflections in the water. Daytime, you can often see mirror images of the buildings. But come night, the buildings disappear and only the lights remain. In the water you see the pattern of lights, some dim, some bright, some white, some yellow, some differing colours. This looks like impressionist art.

The wind created by the speed of the ferry washed over me. I found it a refreshing touch after a hectic day.

The day actually began on the ferry, heading the other direction. I was headed towards the city centre, with the airport as my destination. I had been shooting a series of video messages on the first three chapters of Genesis. But the speaker had to travel to another city. Today, he was travelling back. My morning task was to meet him at the airport and conduct him back home. Our plan was to finish the shoot the same day. We would record four more messages and then he would depart again for Izmir[1]. So, my day began with the rush hour crowds boarding the ferry. On the other side I changed to the tramway, and then to the metro — or underground — to arrive, finally, at the airport.

After meeting the speaker at the airport we travelled back to the flat by the same Metro, tramway and ferry. Once back to the flat, we entered the 'studio'. I say studio, but it used to be called our sitting room/dining room. We shifted the furniture here and there to create a space. This space, temporary though it be, was our studio. The speaker, after a bowl of muesli which we called 'lunch', checked the text on the teleprompter. Then we began shooting. Everything proceeded well until the last message. There was a glitch and we decided to re-shoot it. We had one eye on the clock as we planned to leave at six to make the return trip to the airport. We determined six was the right time to leave to get there on time.

But...

But there was a problem with the text. A couple of lines had been accidentally skipped in the transcribing. So, a hasty correction and we started shooting the last message. The clock ticking. The speaker did an excellent job and we finished taping at six. By the time we were ready to leave, it was 6:30 and the race was on.

When we arrived at the ferry terminal, the doors were mostly shut. But the guardian of the door provided that last minute 'grace' as we flew through the turnstile and ran headlong through the waiting area. We made the ferry!

That was then. And now the speaker was safely delivered to the airport. I completed the metro ride and tramway to the quayside. And now, on the ferry, I was half an hour from home. The reflected lights of the city were dancing on the waters. It was a colourful spectacle and captivating to watch. The night-time reflection turned the most prosaic of industrial complexes into an intriguing pattern of light in the water.

This is what we hope to be — after all the work and labour - to be a reflection of the beauty and glory of God to those around us.

# 22

## September 2004 - It Was a Very Reasonable Desire

The journey started as so many do, with one form of transport to take us to another form of transport. All this to get to go where we wanted to go… We took one of the small motor-ferries to cross the Bosphorus to the wee port of *Kabataş*[1]. There we boarded the much larger ferry that would, well, ferry us to near our destination.

The ferry departed and we sailed serenely on the azure blue waters of the sea of Marmara. The sun was shining and no clouds scurried across the sky.

When we arrived, the ferry disgorged its cargo of day-trippers like us. Like us, but with a difference. I suspect they knew what they were doing and how to go about doing it. I can't confess to knowing what or how to do what we were doing.

Our desire was simple enough — but we were unclear how to accomplish it.

This was our first ever foray to the Princes' Islands. The islands form a wee cluster, nested under the Asian side of Istanbul in the Sea of Marmara.

The Princes' Islands[2]

As we stood on the quay, I mused that the next major earthquake predicted for Istanbul will occur around here. There is an earthquake fault somewhere under these islands.

Well, so they say. Have a nice day on this wee island.

Oh, and they say this 'big' one will happen sometime within the next 30 years.

Now 'Big Island' — so named as it is the biggest of the islands — allows no private motor vehicles. There are no private cars, buses, minibuses or taxis. All are banned.

So, how does one get about the island? Well, Shanks's pony - or the real thing. There are many *faytons*[3]. These horse-drawn carriages will take you where you want to go — for a price.

No motorised vehicles meant it was quiet - you could hear the birds singing in the trees. The island was quaint and gentle. It was very desirable and compelling.

But on this day we were on a quest of a different sort. We did not come to 'discover' or 'explore' the island. Our youngest son, Yusuf, and his then girlfriend were visiting from the UK. As he was born whilst we were living in Turkey, we gave him both an English and a Turkish name — hence Yusuf.

Yusuf had expressed his wish for the day: '*All I want is a nice beach*'. This is a fair enough desire. It is a reasonable goal. There was a small motor boat tied up on the quay. There was a sign declaring its destination was a beach. It seems the boat ride was free, but there was an entrance fee for the beach. This entrance fee included the lounge chairs, umbrella and showers.

Like too many things in Turkey, the fee was not set but was nego-tiable. And to put me at a disadvantage, I was negotiating for some-thing sight unseen. So we will pay whatever I can barter the price down to. I did not know what the 'going rate' would be.

So I bartered and haggled. This is contrary to my temperament and character — but I had no choice. I struggled to find an agreeable sum that would be in the right ball park. I did not want to pay something too high and we would feel ripped off, or too low and we would be left standing on the quayside.

Ah.

After the price was agreed, we boarded the boat, reclining in the aft section – and began our wait. It was a lovely day, the island rising before us, the stretch of Istanbul across the water filling our horizon. The gentle slap of the waves against the side of the boat created a soothing sensation. We were not too bothered by the opportunity to exercise gracious patience in the face of circumstances not quite of our choosing.

Then, we were off....

The boat headed off to where we did not know. We had never been here before. The boat ploughed its way through the sea, doggedly, reluctantly it seemed, around the island. Gradually the town clinging to the edge of the island fell aft of us. We made our way around the island, sailing sou'-sou'-west. The sea was quite calm and there was very little rocking motion. The island slowly passed off the port side. We were, uh, serenaded, by the dulcet throbs of the marine diesel chugging away beneath our feet.

As we progressed around the island I noted with growing concern the lack of 'beaches'. The rocks plunged down rather abruptly into the sea, offering rather picturesque bays but frightfully few beaches. My son reiterated his simple desire for a plain beach. I knew we were going to a beach – but I began to wonder… The word that I was translating as 'beach', Turkish '*plaj*' – well, maybe…

We rounded the corner and the boat nosed into a broad bay, swinging by large fishing trawlers at anchor and sailing past some rather expensive looking pleasure craft. I noted with interest two things. A large boat, larger than the one we were on, a passenger boat, was moored and people were swimming off the deck. The second thing I noted was the eventual destination of our boat. I saw umbrellas. I saw lounge chairs. I saw a restaurant. I saw a place to dock the boat. I saw water. What I did not see was 'sand'. The lounge chairs were on a concrete pad which came to the water and ended in a concrete wall.

Now it never occurred to me to ask the chap I had so patiently negotiated our entrance fee with, if the *plaj* had sand. I assumed that beach meant sand – not a place to swim, with shore facilities to lie in the sun, or shade according to one's tastes.

This was a 'beach' but of the 'sand-less' variety. Words can mean one thing to one person and carry a different meaning to another.

Likewise, as we seek to communicate Good News, we must be aware that words may mean one thing to me but could mean another thing to the hearers. If something as simple and mundane as 'beach' can be misconstrued, then how much more carefully need we to be in our communication. And even more so when speaking of the nature of God, His love, and how we can have a relationship with Him.

# 23

# January 2005 - Snow, a
# Blessing in Disguise

Tülin gazed out the window at a sunny Sunday morning. The opposite shore of the Bosphorus Strait was glistening in the early morning light.

However, when it was time to leave for the morning meeting, the clouds had descended. As we gazed out now, a strong north wind was howling down the Strait. The snow, yes, snow was driving horizontally past the window. We bundled up in gloves, hats, scarves, coats and grabbed an umbrella. The umbrella was not something Tülin would have normally used, but she thought it would help keep some snow off her.

As we stepped out, there was the crunch of snow. This was an unfamiliar experience. There must have been six or seven centimetres of accumulation in that short time between our earlier appreciation of the Bosphorus and our departure. The good thing was that there was little to no traffic. All sensible people were warm and cosy inside.

Ah, where were we?

By the time we arrived at the ferry terminal, my glasses were covered over in wet snow. I couldn't see Tülin. However, even with her umbrella held like a shield in front of her, she was only marginally drier. My front was covered in snow from head to toe. And, of course, I had no snow on my back. We were surprised to see a ferry quayside — looking like it was tucked up with nowhere to go. We quickly learned the large ferries were not running. Why?

Because of the weather.

These large ships, with the capacity of 550 – 700 passengers, were safely nestled up to the quay, draped in snow. So we moved to the next quay, where the smaller motorboats with a capacity of 100 – 250 passengers ply the same route.

They were running. I thought it strange, very strange indeed. The large ferries were not running because of the foul weather. But the little motor boats were carrying on... We bought our ticket and boarded for the quick hop across the Strait. The boat was not crowded. Again, sensible people were still tucked up in their beds. Or maybe observing the weather from the comfort of a soft chair, gazing out of the window with a hot cup of tea in their hands.

At the church, we found some people there. But the foul weather was going to have an impact and the number of those who would make it in. On this Sunday, the number of saints would be diminished. At first I thought that was a shame as we had a guest speaker from Scotland sharing in the morning meeting.

The meeting would start late. So, we had a nice warm cup of tea to take the chill off. The journey had been uneventful, but we were chilled.

Before the meeting many of the saints gathered for prayer in the meeting room. By the end of the prayer time we were running about half an hour later than usual. As we got up to get ready for the meeting, we saw a group of people at the back of the room. They had been there about five minutes. They had waited until the prayer time was done.

A short, stout man was standing about two metres in front of the other visitors. The prayer meeting had broken up and people were scattered all around the room. The stout man began talking; his deep baritone voice filled the room. The tone was direct, forceful, and not friendly. As he talked, the edge in his voice became more hostile.

My Turkish impeded my understanding of all of what he was saying. But I could tell it was unpleasant. Then there was the repeated statement that he was prepared to give his life and take life. This made it clear that he was making a most serious threat.

He spoke. He made his statement. He made his threat. He then gathered the others — his family, it transpired — and departed.

It seems he felt he was owed money by the church. He was threatening people with death if he didn't get what he felt he deserved.

He struck me as one who was not cohabiting in the same reality as me. He, I believed, was living in a reality of his own creation. It may have been one which had been or was being influenced by demons. Either way you cut it, not a pleasant situation.

Now the kicker.

This fellow was once part of the fellowship. He once broke bread with the saints, once taught from the Word. In the past he once carried responsibilities in the fellowship. Now he was threatening people. And it was reported he had joined an Islamic extremist sect.

The guest speaker, who shared a bit later in the morning, did not know what was going to transpire on the day. But God did. The word he gave was extremely appropriate to the events of the day. The passage drew our focus back to actual reality. Our focus was drawn to He who is our Lord and why we are here.

The snow, too, was a blessing. The witnesses to the event were fewer than would have been expected had there been no snow. And the delay was a blessing - his statement was made before the actual meeting. The snow was also a barrier to any visitors who would inquire as to what we believe. Indeed, such a scene could have been a stumbling block to them.

There is a *spiritual battle* going on and it is serious. People have received death threats from credible sources. The Church is being shaken. But God...

But God is sovereign and God is not taken by surprise. But God is with us 'until the end of this age'. God knew the man would come and God knew his words would have an impact. He could have stopped the man from coming, but didn't. He prepared the guest speaker. The speaker was completely ignorant of the man, his history, and that he would come and make threatening demands. And so Sovereign God encouraged us with a word from a man who was outside the situation.

But God...

# 24

# January 2005 - A Most Foreboding Sight

The colour of the Bosphorus Strait reflects the changing moods of the sky. One day it may be a deep, almost black, blue. On another it may be a light, cheery sky blue and on another, a rich turquoise blue.

Today, as I looked out, the Bosphorus was a deep steel-grey colour. The surface was broken by short choppy waves with sporadic white caps. The clouds were dark grey, bordering on black.

The clouds hung low and brooding. The scene looked ominous and a palpable sense of foreboding hung pregnant in the air. It was self evident; soon there would be an onslaught. The wind, would be driven down from the north, assaulting the house. It would howl through the balcony railings like some tormented beast.

Glancing to the north, up the strait towards the Black Sea, there was a large rain cloud. Like a battleship of old, it straddled the channel. In the middle of the channel it stealthily moved downstream and as it came, rain was escaping from the bottom of the cloud. The rain formed great white sheets, reaching from the bottom of the clouds to the troubled surface of the water. It obscured everything in its path.

*Storm clouds over the Bosphorus*

As it reached us, the opposite shore vanished from sight. Like a switch all became engulfed in a grey world of cold, rain, and wind. The house shook, the waters descended. We could see nothing out of the windows but rain and grey clouds, to the accompaniment of the tormented gale.

It slowly passed, plodding onwards. It seemed intent on assaulting the old city to the south. The squall passed. Slowly, as if our vision were returning, we could see the opposite shore. It was slowly escaping from the long, white tendrils of falling rain. The ferries - which never stopped - were once more visible, plying their assigned routes in the sea. Life was going on during the storm and was again in sight before us.

Days before, we had returned to Istanbul. On the trip from the airport to our flat, we asked a Turkish brother who had met us how things were in our absence. I was not in the least prepared for his response.

Christmas may be a non-event in Turkey, but it is meaningful to the Turkish church. For Christmas, they wanted to offer New Testaments on the streets. They asked for and gained permission.

And so, in December, Christians went onto the streets of the three largest cities in Turkey. They offered New Testaments to whosoever wanted one. Some 54,500 New Testaments were given away. This was all legal. The police were present to ensure the freedom of those distributing the New Testaments. Great! Praise the Lord! Wonderful!

The New Testaments were simply offered; whoever wanted one could take one. No one was required to take one. Yet the response to this had been dramatic.

A multitude of incendiary articles said it was a great offence for the Christians to be giving out New Testaments. A flurry of newspaper articles, often front page, followed in its wake. Each one condemning the perceived insult caused. The New Testament project became a cause célèbre. Negative TV programmes were made. Most of the coverage was untrue. All of it seemed designed to incite people's emotions and arouse much heat and smoke. There was heat and smoke, but precious little light.

How has the church responded to this virulent tide of hatred? Some were threatened and others intimidated by the coverage.

Now, nearly a month after the distribution, I have before me three magazines. They serve as samples of what has been put forward in the press. One, on the front page, has the title 'What is the Goal of the Missionaries?' Accompanying the text is a full colour, nine page spread. There are photos of a church, elders, people, books, maps and comments by both believers and Islamic experts.

The headlines were controversial: 'The Missionaries's Plan for Turkey.'

They begin by saying that there are 33 thousand house churches and 55 thousand believers – *oh, **we wish it were true**!* And they claim we stuff dollars in New Testaments - and, according to them, we have distributed 8 million so stuffed!

The article is laced with errors. The author attempts to present our practices and beliefs. But he is presenting his own assumptions of our practices and beliefs. He does not know it, but he is in error. And the picture he paints is an ugly caricature of who and what we are and believe.

There is a storm raging. Visibility is obscure and rain is driving down. Our ears are filled with the howling of the wind. And yet, life goes on. You cannot see, you cannot move, and you cannot act as you did before the storm.

This storm will pass but not just yet.

All the saints have felt the hostile attention — foreign and local believers alike. This has shaken the church. But as winter storms come and then pass, so too this current bout of frenetic activity will pass. As we weather the storm, we find refuge and trust in the Lord. In Him we can rest and be ever ready to give the reason for the hope that we have.

And also, as the Lord Jesus taught, we need to be ever ready to pray for our enemies. To be ready to pray for those who speak ill of us with no cause and for those who do not know or understand us. We pray for the ill-informed, for those who actively oppose us and wish our demise.

Jesus said, '***If your enemy is thirsty, give him a drink***.' Our desire is for those who oppose us the most, that they will taste and drink and drink deeply of the Fountain of Life, that Well of Living Water.

# 25

# April 2005 - No Way am I Going to

I do not have a good memory. It is not just an 'age' thing - I never have had a good memory.

But this was one of those memories that sticks with you. Although it happened in the mid-1970s, I remember it well. We were driving our red VW Beetle down a desolate two-lane highway. This highway cut a straight line through unending forests of northern — *and I mean 'northern'* — Alberta, Canada.

It was the main road to the Peace River country. But in those days it was not a busy road.

Whenever we traversed it, which we had done several times, we met with very little traffic in either direction. On this trip we had the road to ourselves. It was just us, our VW Beetle, and a clear empty road cutting across a vast and inhospitable wilderness. As I mentioned, this was in the mid-1970s and VWs were renowned for their fuel economy. Mind you, by today's standards that 'fuel economy' would be considered rather profligate. But in those days it was the best there was. I loved seeing how far I could go on a tank of petrol. The trip itself was what I considered a short 600 mile hop

(965 kilometres). That was then, now I considered that not just a long journey, but a two-day journey!)

We had been driving for several hours and, slowly but surely, the petrol gauge was making its way, inexorably, toward the E on the dial. The time was drawing nigh to when the fuel endurance test would be at its completion. It was clear, we should find a petrol station.

Now this was a fairly tedious section of the highway. The forest was not of lofty pines, but of scrub pines. There were dreary pockets of stagnant water and jagged rocks. The land was uninhabited and for a reason.

And for this very reason petrol stations were not around every corner. In fact, there weren't many corners on this road. It ran straight as a die, undulating over a seemingly never-ending series of low hills. Each hill cleft by the ribbon of road with hidden low valleys between. Hidden until it was revealed when we broached the crest of the hill.

Invariably, the vista was the same; the road dropping straight down the gentle incline of the hill, then across the valley floor, and gently curving straight up the opposite side. Rarely did we see a sign. It was rare to come across a reminder of another world other than this monotonous line through the bush. Rarer still was a petrol station.

Finally, we arrived at the first petrol station we had seen in miles and miles. I pulled in, hot, dusty and a bit bone weary from the trip. I brought the car to a stop in front of the pump and glanced over at the price. This was in the days when petrol was sold by the gallon, none of this litre stuff. The normal price for a gallon of petrol was about 49 Canadian cents. But the price on this pump, in the middle of nowhere, was a princely 70 cents a gallon — Canadian.

My eyes bulged out.

I sputtered and babbled.

One glance at the petrol gauge and the position of the needle hovering slightly above the 'E'.

'No way,' I exclaimed with true vehemence. I added, 'No way am I going to pay 70 cents. 70 CENTS for a gallon of petrol!!!'

And with that one forceful statement muttered to no one in particular, I started the car up. The fuel endurance test entered a new phase as we pulled out of the station and headed off into the wilderness.

Sitting in Istanbul in 2005, a nostalgic sigh slips unbidden from my lips. I've just returned from fuelling up the car. The price of a litre of petrol here is only ₺2.53 — Turkish lira. This is roughly £1 or about $2.31 Canadian or $1.87 US a litre. Now, to put this in perspective, if you are like me and still relate best to a gallon amount, that works out to £4.55 or $10.50 Canadian for an Imperial gallon or $7.08 US for an American gallon.

I repent! I repent with all my heart. Please bring back the 70 cent gallon!

But those days are, I'm afraid, gone. And they are gone for good.

Sometimes it is difficult to see things in perspective. But strive we must, and in all things, and I mean all things, be thankful. Often we find it quite challenging to be thankful.

There are many situations where we feel it is not possible or even reasonable to be thankful. Sometimes it is jolly hard to be thankful, but in the fullness of time, it may be very possible to be truly thankful. There are other times when, even after the passage of time, we still find it is still not be possible to be thankful.

But if we focus on the good, the positive lessons learned, we may be thankful. I found an Internet page which contained an interview with Michael J. Fox - a North American actor. It was fascinating, uplifting and incredibly challenging. In the interview he declared he is thankful for his Parkinson's disease. This disease cut short a career he loved and yet, *he says*, it has changed him into a better person.

But consider the One who loves us to the point of giving His one and only Son that we may live. At the end of all things this is something we can be profoundly thankful for. This is a constant, regardless of whatever may befall us.

# 26

# May 2005 - Of Churches and Churches

M y head was pounding. And my eyes ached and yearned to be shut. My tummy, normally very receptive to food, was now quietly rebelling. Everything told me it was time to stop and rest.

But.....

But this was the one day — singular — we would be in Diyarbakır. Ah, Diyarbakır; a city in eastern Turkey on the banks of the Tigris River. Most of the ancient core of the city is still surrounded by walls build of the local black basalt stones. It is impressive, intimidating even. The roots of this city go back to antiquity. It was known as Amida in Roman times. And today was our *one* chance to collect some stock video footage of the old quarter.

The previous day, we had driven from Nevşehir[1]. We crossed mountains and passed spectacular snow-capped peaks. Our path took us through green valleys and down narrow gorges. We even travelled along the rim of a great canyon.

In my youth, I had read about the fertile crescent. I was engrossed with the stories of the mighty Tigris and Euphrates rivers. Our plan for the next day would take us down to the shores of the Tigris River.

There we would see a city built into the stone of a massive cliff. Soon everything in the valley we would see, including the ancient stone bridge crossing the Tigris, was to be inundated because of a new dam.

From there, we would travel to the city of Midyat. And leaving Midyat, we would carry on to a small village. Why? It is the last **all Aramean**[2] village left in Turkey. They still speak Aramaic — the language of Jesus.

There we would be hosted by a believer and his extended family. We would be there for one night. This would be a rare opportunity for them as there are no like-minded believers in their village. The local church is a Syrian Orthodox church. The family rarely meet with evangelical believers. This would be a time to receive some teaching and to celebrate the Lord's Supper.

Therefore, if we were to film the city, *today* was the day. So, feeling well or not, I wanted to do it. For filming, I took the smaller video camera, a tripod, and a still camera. Oh, and the leader of the local church sent two Turkish believers with us. They were to be our guides *and protectors*. The old city is awash with a sea of street children.

Throbbing head, camera over my shoulder and eyes squinting in the sunlight, we headed off to the first site of the day. We were being guided to an old church called Surp Sarkis. This was an Armenian church.

The abandoned church was surrounded by a three metre high cement block wall with a steel bar gate. The gate was locked. Through the bars we could see a large concreted courtyard and the massive stone church anchored on one side.

We knocked on the gate for the watchman. Nothing. We, as two foreigners, attracted the attention of the locals. One neighbour, to be helpful, told our Turkish guides the watchman was away. She did not know when he would return…

So, we resolved to video through the gate and be content with that. Back I trudged to the gate, lugging the gear with me, head pounding, tummy complaining. I aimed the camera through the bars and then someone suggested I mount the gate and shoot over the top. Okay, a good idea, I would get a much better shot.

*This was the gate I climbed*

Throbbing head notwithstanding, I scrambled up the steel facade of the gate. When my head topped the gate, I called for my camera. I framed the church through the eyepiece of the camera. It was then we were told it was okay to climb over the gate if we wished. So, down came the camera and I hoisted myself over the top of the gate.

Now I'm of short stature. So, at the top of the gate, when I swung my leg over the top, I couldn't actually reach the crossbar. The steel gate wobbled uncomfortably. So, by faith, I released my tenuous hold on something remotely firm and swung my body over the top — following my yet unsecured leg — over the gate. There I searched frantically for the crossbar as my weight crossed the apex of the gate. After finding the crossbar, I continued my descent. The camera and tripod were handed to me through the bars of the gate. I headed off towards the church.

Strangely, my headache was now gone. This would not be an easy cure to bottle.

I started my collection of stock footage of the church. I entered the structure – most of the roof had collapsed. I was walking on the remains of the logs that had stretched from stone wall to stone wall. The layer of dirt that had formed the flat earthen roof was now beneath my feet. The humps and bumps of dirt formed an uneven surface which masked the original floor and floor covering.

As I set up for a series of shots inside the building, I heard a noise behind me. I turned to see Tülin with the still camera taking shots of the building. Now I knew she did not have a headache — which would need my new found cure. So how did she get here? I could not imagine her climbing over the gate in her long skirt.

While I was busy in the ruins, the watchman had returned. He opened a more prosaic door for my companions to use.

*The ruins of a large church in Diyarbakır*

The carcass of the church, built around 1500 AD, was made of finely fitted stones. Inside there were rounded stone arches. There were rows and rows of simple but impressive stone pillars. They were topped by plain capitals. Perched on top of the pillars were grand arches, creating a large open space for the people to gather. There were simple stone carvings dotted within the structure.

The steel rings which would have supported the lighting system remained at the apex of the arches.

After the roof had collapsed, the wind, rain and frost had free rein. I was overwhelmed by the thought that soon this stark ruin will disappear. Once it was a building in full use. Now the floor is hidden under the debris. Slowly these impressive remains will crumble and fall. In time, nothing recognisable will remain.

A few days later, we arrived in Antakya. This is the modern name for the city. In ancient times it was called Antioch but there were many Antiochs. Which one was this? The one on the Orontes river. It was here the followers of the Way were first called Christians. And it was here the church commissioned Barnabas and Saul to the First Missionary Journey.

And now, here we were gathered with a small group of believers.

This Sunday morning we approached the building via a narrow, almost medieval street. We came to a blank wall with a plain steel door.

Passing through the door to this old stone house, we came first to a stone courtyard. This separated the room for the meeting on the left from an office-cum-Sunday School room, a sitting room, kitchen and toilet on the right. Although the courtyard was long and narrow, there was a lemon, an orange, a pomegranate and a medlar tree. They all conspire to provide shade, a sweet aroma, and fruit in season.

There were fewer people there than normal. Most of the ladies had travelled to Adana for the annual ladies' conference[3].

But here was a small group of believers with local leadership. They lifted their voices in songs of worship, praising, and praying to the Lord. Together we spent time in the Word of God.

Now here was the real Church, not a collection of stones. A simple gathering of saints, praising the Lord, loving Him, loving one another and learning together. The time with these saints was precious indeed.

The leader of the fellowship works for the Department of Health and he is also the elder. He is alone in leadership and he challenged me to consider moving to this city to assist him.

In this land, dotted with the ruins of ancient churches, this was a breath of fresh air, reminding me of what our life is all about. Our focus is not on the opposition or the flash-bang grenade attacks that had occurred recently. Nor were we focused on the character assignations and the misrepresentation of our calling.

Our focus is on our Sovereign Lord building His Church. And it is about the fact that the Gates of Hell shall not prevail against it.

This land is liberally dotted with the ruins of former church buildings. They stand as silent testimony that once the Living Church was abundant across this region. Today there are new fellowships being created. The Living Church is rising. And the buildings they use are simple and unimpressive. The life they live is breath-taking. They show a simple faith and trust in the God of the universe.

# 27

# June 2005 - The Journey of a Lifetime

During winter, the town of *Kuşadası*[1] is a sleepy little backwater. But come the tourist season, it is a thriving, bustling hive of activity. It is on the Aegean coast, close to ancient Ephesus.

On this holiday we were joined by some dear friends — we made a party of four. We have known our friends for many years, sharing a love and passion for the Turks and Turkey. They were also joint owners of our flat in Istanbul. It was large enough for them to have the lower floor and we upstairs. Upstairs was a small, self-contained granny flat. It was wee but had a magnificent view of the Bosphorus. Hence we shared the same flat - but lived separately.

On the day we arrived in *Kuşadası* was a large luxury liner, *MSC Opera*, in port. The quay was two sided; on the one side was the towering hulk of the cruise ship and opposite was the wee island hopper we were taking to the Greek island of Samos. The difference was greater than large and small. It was more like a night and day difference.

Speaking with a chap on the quayside, he informed us it would cost $5,000 (USD) for eight days on the luxury liner. I think that was per person! For me, that is a lot for a big steel hotel that moves.

Our goal was not Samos but Patmos. However, we had been told that there was no onward ferry from Samos to Patmos that day. We had planned to spend one night on Samos before continuing our journey. This would not be a hardship.

However, on arrival at the port on Samos, we learned that indeed there was a ferry to Patmos that day. We also learned it was a hydrofoil, which means fast. And it was from the port of Pythagoreio[2]. Pythagoreio was on the other side of the island. We hastily arranged for a taxi to take us over to the port whence the hydrofoil sailed.

We topped the pass and saw down below us the wee town, a bay and the hydrofoil. It was sitting in a picturesque harbour. From the harbour you could easily see across the narrow strait separating Samos from Turkey. The hydrofoil wasn't large; it was brightly painted and lying low in the water like any normal boat. It was called a flying dolphin.

The departure time came. But because it was May, the tourist season hadn't really started and so there were but a few people on board. The hydrofoil parted company with the quay and made its way out of the harbour. It turned and headed south towards the Greek island of Patmos.

As we were leaving the harbour and making our way out, we sailed through a cluster of sail boats; some of their number were heading south and others north from Pythagoreio. At first, as they exited the harbour, they were under motor power and later, when free in the Aegean, under sail.

As our ship picked up speed, it gently lifted out of the water, leaving the friction of the ship's bottom clear of the water as she sped along. She was held high by special struts extending down into the water with distinctive foils. It was these extraordinary foils that held the bulk of the ship out of the water. It was like the ship was skiing. This increased the speed of the ship by reducing drag.

We went to the front passenger space. The forward window curved round. This provided a full view forward of the ship. It was a tremendous panorama unfolding before us. Travelling south swinging southwest, we travelled down the east coast of the island of Samos, the barren rocky mountain sides plunging down into the sea, occasionally as dramatic cliffs.

We continued our journey in the Aegean and, in time, encountered large luxury cruise ships making the passage between Samos and Turkey. There was a series of them, almost like a wagon train making its way across the surface of the sea. Soon Kuşadası would be crowded with more ships like the *MSC Orient*.

Thankfully, the sea was calm, like a mill pond, and so provided a smooth surface for the hydrofoil to rise and fly. It was only occasionally that the gentle swell would cause a heaving motion, a bit to the right, a bit to the left, a bit up. There was nothing spectacular, but enough to remind you that you are on the sea.

To the left – uh, I guess I should say port. Er, unless it is starboard, hmm, better say left. To the left, through the murky haze, the indistinct form of an island slowly resolved into view. Unclear, not far off, but forever like a dream or a phantom – there, but not really.

*Our flying dolphin...*

As we swayed and rode through the sea, our peace was disturbed by an odd sound. No idea what it was, but they slowed down a bit. We never sussed out what it was.

When I say we slowed down, we were still flying right along and we caught up with one of the luxury liners, gracefully making her way southward. They may travel in style, but we would get there long before them.

Again off to our left, two freighters hove into view, ploughing north-ward. They were possibly going to a Greek island, Izmir, Istanbul, or the Black Sea. Their destination, like our mystery island, which we almost saw, was hidden from us. Their hulls were below the hori-zon, with only their upper decks coming into view.

Halfway into this one hour hop – the same journey is four hours by normal ferry – another form gradually came into view, now on the right side. And another. And off to the west, not yet revealing its form, the hint of another island. There were hidden depths and places that we were flying past.

The hydrofoil slowed, and the ship settled back into the water for a slow cruise into Skala, the port on Patmos. On arrival, we were greeted by a lady who was, in broken English, inviting us to examine her self-catering accommodation.

So we did. It looked ok – but I wanted to see if there was something better in Chora. Chora is perched on the very top of a high hill. It looks down on all sides. Patmos is not a large island. Chora is the main town, with great views and envelopes the monastery. If there was an accommodation up there, I wanted to know…

Without booking the room we looked at, we went back to the town centre. It was there I discovered I had left my PIM[3] in the room when we looked at it. (A PIM was a device in 2005 that was like a poor tablet or Chromebook. This was in the time before smart phones, iPads and such.)

One of our travelling companions, Roger, went to find the lady to find my PIM. Yvonne opted to go back to the place we had just looked at. Tülin sat down and watched the luggage, and I rented a motorbike to zip up to Chora and 'check it out'.

So off I roared on the two wheeled thunderbolt and followed the winding road up the mountain to Chora. At the top the town spread over the summit and spilled down the sides, and I did not know where I was going. So, I took a random turn, then a hairpin to a higher street, and finally I entered the maze of medieval streets that is Chora. One narrow lane led to another, followed by turns here and there. I was always on the lookout for any accommodation. Often I was looking for a street wide enough for a car -- and not finding one. And slowly, I worked my way in deeper. I went winding my way further without finding anything.

Then things got awkward. I wasn't finding any accommodation and now I couldn't find my way out.

One street ended at a dead end. Another took me to the monastery. The monastery looked more like a castle to me. And another 'road' was too narrow for the motorbike(!). And still another one that ended in stairs.

What to do?

Slowly, I made my way back through the maze. I found a way out and broke free from the grip of some medieval street planner.

I think this was one line of defence. If an enemy comes into the town to attack the monastery, he may get lost in the streets.

Anyway, I was found, I was free, back on a road that was wider than the motorcycle. And so I headed back.

And then the engine faltered. What was this? Don't know, but it was working fine. And now it had stopped. And it wouldn't start.

So, as it was virtually all downhill, off I went, silent in the sun. I cruised down the hill, around the hairpin curves, past the Cave of the Apocalypse to the town at the bottom.

I pushed the bike into the shop. On getting a replacement, I also had a stern exhortation to go buy some petrol. This I promptly did.

We decided where we would stay. As there didn't appear to be any accommodation in Chora, we would take the first place we looked at. Ah...ah...

Later in the evening, after spending more money that we didn't really have for the evening repast, we sat on the ample terrace. This terrace was shared between the two rooms. We chatted with our holiday companions over a cup of tea.

Amazing. Yesterday we were in Istanbul! Wow! One day in Istanbul, the next in Patmos, sitting on a terrace enjoying the view and a cup of tea.

Yes, there had been a lot of driving, two different ferries and we were here – and yet, still probably in less time than it took John to come here from nearby Ephesus...

# 28

# June 2005 - In Search of John

The new day dawned with some high, wispy clouds. They were left over from the rainstorm in the night, depositing some puddled water on the terrace. Our breakfast was a leisurely affair — we were on holiday after all.

Then we set about the business of the day — to return to where I saw the sign to the Cave of the Apocalypse. So, Tülin and I mounted our motorcycle for the day's adventures.

The last book of the Bible, Revelation, was written by the Apostle John on the island of Patmos. That was the allure that brought us to this Greek island. John, a follower of Jesus, spent the latter years of his life living in Ephesus. It was while in Ephesus that he was exiled to Patmos. Whilst there, he received the revelation of Jesus Christ that is described in the book of Revelation. As the book describes the end of the age and the end of the world, it is also referred to as the Apocalypse.

*The entrance to the Monastery of the Cave of the Apocalypse*

But where on this small island did John receive his vision, and where did he write the book? Well, the Greek Orthodox Church has an answer.

The Monastery of the Cave of the Apocalypse was not far out of town. It was halfway up the hill between the port town of Skala, and Chora on the summit. I had set out to video much of the island and so, after we parked up, I unloaded and lugged the kit. There was a still camera, video camera, tripod, and other paraphernalia. The main door led to a corridor and room from which we exited to the left or north. We traipsed across a small courtyard, down some stairs, past a chapel. Then, down some more stairs, around a corner, and down some more stairs. Finally, we entered a small chapel and to the side there was a smaller chapel in a cave. There was no dividing wall between the two chapels and they seemed to merge into one.

*This is the door that leads to the cave (no photos allowed inside)*

Prominently displayed was a symbol sign saying no photos and no video. Now, we could have tried but didn't — doing the right thing is not related to your chances of getting away with doing the wrong thing. Leaving the formal chapel in the front, we entered the cave proper. There was a low rock ceiling. Even a short person like me had to duck to enter. There were two low benches near the front.

On the right there was a naturally occurring rock shelf, and a cordoned off space near a round hole carved in the wall. This had a decorative horseshoe-shaped silver decoration. This was said to be the place where John had laid his head. Part way up the wall was an indentation that was likewise surrounded in a silver decorative band. It was said to be a handhold to help John get up. The rock shelf, they said, was the place where a scribe wrote what John dictated to him.

At the very front there was a wooden divider. It was behind this divider the priest would perform his various duties. The wall was decorated with many paintings, including one which was a picture of the first chapter of Revelation.

I examined every nook and cranny that seemed to be allowed, even looking behind the dividing partition, as looking seemed to be okay. We didn't light a candle, but Roger read the first chapter of the book of Revelation. During his reading, an older couple came in. The man went forward to a painting and kissed it. Then he and the lady accompanying him sat down. Roger asked if they minded him reading and they seemed pleased he was — so he continued.

There is no reason to think that this was the place the revelation was revealed — and likewise, no reason to doubt it either.

After this we boarded our petrol-powered steeds and went up to Chora. For me, this was to go back into the medieval streets. However, this time I had purpose and direction. Our goal was the monastery at the very top.

We flew along the narrow cobbled paths. If I said 'streets', it would give a totally false impression — these were narrow, er, paths. My tripod, normally content to sit in front of me on the motorcycle, began a slow but determined drift off to one side. I said, 'oh-oh' and floored it. Our goal, which we were pressing on towards, was in sight. We arrived, stopped, and the tripod slipped off. Perfect timing.

The timing was perfect, but my navigation was not. Whilst I guided us to our goal, we were nearer the back door than the front. Igno-

rance is bliss, so the saying goes. I had come the long way around —
well, it was scenic. We left the bikes, took all the gear once again,
walked around to the front door and entered the monastery. It looks
like a fortress. Indeed, it was built like this for a purpose.

When the monastery was founded in 1088, the island was deserted.
This was because of the effective work of pirates. So when the
Greek Orthodox priests returned, they built the monastery to with-
stand the intensive interest of passing pirates.

The monastery inside the massive stone walls was a warren. There
were rooms, chapels, churches, kitchens, ancillary rooms, treasury,
library and I do not know what the other rooms were. We looked in
the churches. My eyes were drawn first to the no photography, no
video symbol signs. Then I followed my feet up stairs and down
corridors, freely going anywhere that wasn't blocked by a simple
gate, door or sign. We descended to the door to the treasury. This is
now a museum. However, the €6 entry price put me off — you
cannot do everything or go everywhere. There was a priest there, so
I started chatting with him. He said the island was inhabited with
towns until the 7th century, when it was abandoned because of
pirates. Abandoned, until the founding of the fortress monastery in
1088.

*A view from the monastery in Chora*

So, when John was exiled here, there were people and towns.

He told me they had, in their extensive library, over 1000 manuscripts, plus 30,000 other books. Their oldest manuscript dated to the 5th century! It was of the whole Bible. They had made a copy of their oldest manuscript. They copied their pages, the other pages in Russia and England, and produced a facsimile of the complete manuscript. It was on offer for €360. I would have loved to buy a copy! If I had €360, I would have bought it immediately. But, given I had not entered the Treasury because of the princely entrance fee of €6, there wasn't much chance of me affording this book — however much I wanted it. I thought it might be useful in sharing with people who say the Bible has been changed.

Anyway, we left and returned to our lodging to have lunch.

# 29

# June 2005 - Over the Hills and Dales

*Getting about on a small island*

Day two of our time on Patmos. For our morning outing we went to a place near to our residence. It was a short motor-bike ride away… Or so it seemed.

But, one turn led to another. We were trying to follow signs for the acropolis[1].

### Acropolis

From Wikipedia, the free encyclopedia

*For other uses, see Acropolis (disambiguation).*
*See also: Acropolis of Athens*

An **acropolis** (Ancient Greek: ἀκρόπολις, akropolis, from akros (ἄκρος) or akron (ἄκρον), "highest, topmost, outermost" and polis (πόλις), "city"; plural in English: acropoles, acropoleis or acropolises)[1] was an ancient Greek settlement, especially a citadel, built upon an area of elevated ground --frequently a hill with precipitous sides, chosen for purposes of defense.[2] Acropolises also had a function of a religious sanctuary with sacred springs highlighting its religious significance.[3] Acropolises became the nuclei of large cities of classical antiquity, such as ancient Athens, and for this reason they are sometimes prominent landmarks in modern cities with ancient pasts, such as modern Athens. One well-known acropolis is the Acropolis of Athens, located on a rocky outcrop above the city of Athens and containing the Parthenon.

Wikipedia contributors, "Acropolis", Wikipedia, The Free Encyclopedia, 7 September 2021, 20:56 UTC, <https://en.wikipedia.org/w/index.php?title=Acropolis&oldid=1042966421>

Because the acropolis would have been the central point of any ancient Greek city, I thought that John the Apostle may have been there. Well, it is possible. So, it became the first goal of the day.

We set off following the signs directing us to the acropolis. The last sign turned us up the hill behind Skala. With two of us on the motorbike, I floored it up the narrow concrete path between the houses. We were barrelling up the hill for all we were worth when I noticed that the smooth, steep concrete way had ceased. Where it stopped, the path continued as stairs. Now, I had already managed an earlier spill, so I knew when to stop. I was not up to attempting to ride a motorbike up stairs. So we stopped, parked up, and walked up the stairs.

The stairs led to a dirt track the width of a walking trail. We forged onwards and, truly in this case, upwards.

After a while we arrived at a white painted chapel. These white painted chapels are ubiquitous in Greece. They are even more ubiquitous on the holy island of Patmos. I thought this might lead to where we were going, so we carried on to the chapel.

It didn't.

Yvonne opted to remain in the shade, under blooming trees, and there enjoy the view. The rest of us went back to the track, to carry on further along, and further upwards. As time passed, the trail become less promising. We arrived at a point where it was clear the going was not getting easier. Roger opted to return by the way we came, whilst Tülin and I pressed on. My immediate goal was the edge of the cliff that dropped into the sea. As the acropolis was defensive, I expected to find some ruins there, as it would be an ideal place. Barring that, then there would be a prime vantage point to get some good video of the sea, cliffs and crashing waves. I saw no *identifiable* acropolis but splendid views of the coast and sea.

Then we carried on up the hill to another white chapel. I said they are ubiquitous. Finally, we broached the summit. I tried a 360° panorama, but it didn't work as well as I hoped. I was standing on the top of a loose pile of stones, so did not have the best platform to accomplish this task. On our descent we filmed some dressed stones in situ. This was the most tangible remnant of the ancient city. Or maybe not - dressed stone is impossible for me to date.

*In search of the acropolis*

We went down, joined up with Roger and Yvonne, and returned to our motorbikes. We motored back to our self-catering rooms.

After lunch we motorbiked off to another vantage point for some cliff filming. The best vantage point was part way down the bank. So, I went part way down the bank. I got some good footage, with the tripod set, as per usual, on the edge of a cliff.

*Our primary mode of transportation*

The next destination was a chapel perched on top of a high hill. It was only 225 metres high, but it was one of the highest hills on the island. It was obvious where we were going. It stuck out like, well, a high hill with a white building perched on the very summit. We followed the asphalt road south and wound our way to the base of the hill. There we turned the corner and saw the road that would lead us to the summit. It was a fairly new, *narrow* concrete road. Let me clarify, it was a fairly new, narrow and *extremely steep* concrete road.

Tülin was not over enthusiastic with the prospect of the ascent but stayed on the motorbike. Yvonne opted to rest in the sun there at the bottom and let Roger go up by himself.

Giving the wee motor lots of gas, we were in motion, and before Tülin knew it, we had begun our attempt at attaining the height.

At first, all seemed to go okay. True, there was no guard rail. The roadway was just the width of a car. And it was steep. The engine roared as the bike struggled to carry the two of us, two cameras and Tülin's backpack. Oh, yes, the tripod was also perched on the motorbike as we struggled up the incline. Shortly, we were greeted with the view of the concrete road coming to an end.

'The stupid road ends… It ends… The stupid road ends…' a rather emphatic voice kept shouting in my ear. I could easily hear her despite the roar of the little engine straining to provide sufficient power to keep us moving forward and upward.

It was not the end of the world. Nor, it transpired, was it the end of the road. It was an acute hairpin turn. We had done many hairpins on this island; that wasn't the initial concern. But the scattering of loose stones on the surface was drawing my attention.

'Okay, turn sharp, slow down, but not too slow, avoid the rocks, do not lose momentum and have to stop (fell off last time), stay on the road…'

And we rounded the curve and continued on the course. The incline lessened a wee bit. We felt better for it as we roared onwards, past a bemused couple walking sedately down the hill. Then the next major ascent began. Still no guard rails, still a narrow little concrete way, still extremely steep. And on we flew…

The next hairpin was tight, as was the final one. We roared the final few metres up the slope. I swung into the car park area and, amid the fumes of an overheated little engine, I turned the bike off.

Was the view worth it? Undoubtedly, yes! But the trip was not fun.

Going down, the motor stalled, so we coasted down. No problem.

# 30

# June 2005 - But I Thought it was Back

I n life, we make many little assumptions that help us get on with things. Normally, if we are in error, nothing happens. Well, I made an assumption.

The day dawned with a hazy obscurity about it. We lathered up with sunblock. I wore a long-sleeved shirt and long trousers, with little exposed skin to burn. However, there was still my nose and ears and face and the top of my hands. We headed off to Chora first for some shots of us riding through the labyrinth of streets. That accomplished, we headed off to the north.

The first visit was to the village of St Nicholas — one of the older sites on the island. It dates back to the 11th century. Mind you, there was just a collection of a few houses and nothing that looked even remotely ancient… Maybe the ruins are off to one side somewhere. It was scenic enough. We left there on our way to a morning cup of iced coffee when I saw a side road. I was told I could follow my nose, so off we went. I thought it went to one of the ubiquitous little white chapels.

Well, it did, and more.

The road carried on past the chapel and down to a picturesque bay. Down went the road and there was some agricultural land, very pleasant indeed. Some video taken, and we mounted the motorbike for the climb out. As we passed the chapel, our attention was drawn to a man working in a wheat field. In his hand was a hand scythe and he was scything the wheat and tying sheaves. Would have loved to video that. But I felt the need to ask permission and I did not think he spoke English. Ah well...

After a refreshing cup of iced coffee, we agreed with our travelling companions to go 'to the end of the road'. From my study of the map of the island I knew a wee chapel to St Apollo was on the way. We agreed to take this side trip and visit it.

As I said, there are countless wee chapels dotted all over the countryside and on the small rocky outcrops sitting in the sea. They all have names and their own history. But, alas, there are so many they become part of the wallpaper. They are interesting in their own right — but few people will ever discover their unique story. We were numbered among those who would never know.

Up and down we went until we arrived at the turning - the turning to the gravel road that led down to St Apollo. The gravel road had received some maintenance, but it was still a gravel road. Up we went, over a ridge, and then we began going down towards the coast. It was a gravel road with a steep incline. It was bumpy and rough and off the right side, well, it just went off...

Ahead there was a curve to the left and the road disappeared from view. Our speed was moderate for the road. But it was picking up pace. Tülin was not at all comfortable with either the speed or the fact that the road disappeared from view. She made a request for the speed to be reduced.

Playing the fool, I allowed the speed to increase a bit. Like I said, I was playing the fool. And when she was more adamant that we slow down, I applied ample pressure to what I *'assumed'* was the back brake.

Now if my speed had been less, or if my basic 'assumption' had been correct, all would have been fine. But, alas, my speed was not less and my assumption couldn't have been more inaccurate.

I applied ample pressure to the brake, to the brake I always favoured. I thought I needed to brake with the back brake over the front. Considering the road conditions, angle of descent, and our speed, that was even more important.

However, I was in fact actually favouring the front brake. Therefore, things quickly twisted out of control.

I applied too much front brake, not enough back brake. The front tyre locked up. There was no steerage and the front of the bike was trying to go slower than the back. Motorbikes are not designed for the back to pass the front. As the back tyre attempted to do just that, the motor bike spilled over.

Thankfully, we were on the bank side of the road and not on the cliff side. Thankfully, our speed wasn't all that fast. It felt fast - but in reality, it was not. A sudden, unexpected, unwanted toppling off the bike resulted from my brake management practice.

Down we went. We came to an abrupt halt. The tripod came off. I don't think I landed on the video camera. But my first thought was to the blood on my right hand. I guess I must have reached out with it as we fell off to the left… No mark on my left hand. Now my left leg had something to show for the event. Tülin — *the innocent party* — had a few scrapes on one hand and had landed on her back in the ditch. She was unscathed in this version of my dumping off the bike technique.

Well, nothing appeared broken. So, we carried on further down the hill until after a certain point the road was impassible for any motorised transport. Consequently, we parked up and two of the four walked the remaining distance to the St Apollo Chapel — it was locked.

I went down and washed my hand and leg in the sea and put on some antibacterial cream (Tülin is prepared for all contingencies).

Then, as we had come this far, I took some video. After that, we headed back up the mountain.

*Washing my wounds...*

Once on the crest of the hill, Tülin rejoined me on the bike. Strangely, she had declined the ride up the road. As we began our gradual and controlled descent down the opposite side, I notice the front tyre locking...

**It was at this point the light dawned.**

The left brake was back, **not** front. The right brake was front and **NOT** back. Ah... Ah...

So, I tested this theory. I dynamited the new 'back brake' and the rear tyre stopped moving, and I still had steerage. ***All became clear.*** This was why we tumbled. I favoured the wrong brake, locked up the front tyre and lost steerage.

So, I've learned my lesson, I hope, and I have the marks to show the lesson it was. I must be careful of assumptions - they can hurt!

*Up, up and away...*

In the afternoon we drove over the south part of the island, including a quick trip — sans Tülin — up the highest mountain again. Roger stayed at the bottom. So it was me on my motor and Yvonne on hers. Much easier with just one person on board.

That evening, in the Internet café, there was a sign recruiting extras for a film being shot on the island. We all four volunteered for it. So, the following morning early, very early, we reported as extras — the call sheet called for 6:30. We spent the day on a ferry, basically sitting in the bay — we waited and then filled in the background when required by the director. There was even a helicopter shot with the director continuously exhorting us not to look at the helicopter but at the actors splashing in the sea. Lunch was included. And we were paid €30 each for the pleasure. If you want to watch the movie, it is called Opa! starring Matthew Modine.

And so our time being involved in the filming of Opa! concluded our brief trip to Patmos. For me, it was an ideal holiday. There were no crowds, no parties, no loud noises, just a quiet little island. Ah, bliss…

# 31

# November 2005 - Then the Elder

The journey had started — and it started early. As we drove, I was taken aback by the diversity of the countryside. We travelled through forest, over mountains and across plains.

My appreciation was dulled by the 4 a.m. start. We sighted snow, first on the high, rocky peaks. But our path took us into the interior. There the snow gradually moved closer to the road. For me, this was not a welcome sight. Snow at a distance is great, but not close up! The further we drove, the higher the road went. As we went up, the snow drew closer until it was not too far distant at all.

We drove, steady, for nine and a half hours. We were in the vicinity of the conference centre. In the morning, we were on the shores of the Bosphorus. Come evening, we were on the Mediterranean coast. Neither my travelling companion nor I had been there before. So, we implemented the Turkish proverb, '*sora, sora Bağdat bulunur.*' This means by asking many questions, you will find Baghdad. In plain speech - ask for directions. This was before satnav.

So, we slowly, asking as we went, worked our way along the coast. In the fullness of time, we finally arrived at our destination.

We had been warned beforehand that the hotel was nice. Actually, it was very nice, nicer than we would normally see the inside of. We had been assured that the selection of this hotel resulted from an extremely good off-season deal. We were also told not to feel uncomfortable – despite the surroundings - as it was actually affordable.

The food was abundant, delicious, and catered for most palates. The first language of the meetings was Turkish and the times of worship were all in Turkish. The worship and the teaching were all outstanding.

There were workers, both foreign and local, from all over the country.

Truth be told, I was impressed with the hotel.

There were many foreigners who had come from overseas to be part of the conference. I was glad the organisers had esteemed our Turkish brothers by giving prominence to Turkish.

The focus of the consultation was partnership. The partnership could be in prayer or it could also be in projects, personnel or funding.

As the days progressed, I became quite discouraged, bordering on depressed. Now you can argue that I should not have felt this way. And you can assert believers are not to experience this or feel this way.

But it was the way I was feeling.

Partly, I suppose, it was because of the upset of my normal routine. My normal mid-meal snacks to keep my blood sugar somewhat balanced were missing. When my blood sugar drops, I feel depressed.

Partly, it was from a feeling of competition. There were ministry displays in one room. It was here my travelling companion had set up his display for his Christian publishing house. And here I set up a display of the various Turkish language teaching VCDs we had produced. I guess I should explain that VCDs or Video CDs, were like a DVD but using the cheaper CDs rather than a DVD. The VCDs had less capacity, meaning the video was of lower quality. But this was the most widespread media for any programme to be distributed in Turkey.

It was in this room, shared with many other ministries within Turkey, that I realised it was as if we were all in competition. Each one vying for the interest and attention of the people at the consultation. And by proxy, for the hearts and minds of the saints living in Turkey. It was as if each one of us were saying, '*We have the answer for you.*' Or '*You need what I offer.*' Or '*I have the answer to your problem.*' I am not saying that was happening. I am saying, that is how *I felt* at the time – as I said, '*as if.*'

Hence, I was feeling down. I was asking myself, 'Is it all worth it?'

Distribution had been the challenge for the VCD programmes we had produced. If I joined in with all the others saying, 'Get my programmes, this is what you need,' what would I be saying? I felt like, for me, I would be part of the Great Competition rather than the Great Commission.

Then the elder from a fellowship in Istanbul approached me. He asked me to join him in a meeting with a Turkish couple – I had absolutely no inkling why I should be included.

This couple recounted their pilgrimage. They started with their beginning as traditional conservative folk. They shared, sadly, the events which culminated in the death of their son. Then they elaborated on what developed after that.

Their story included some remarkable experiences. They explained their efforts to cope with the death. And they were seeking answers. They found and read a Bible. At one point they travelled to a church and in the course of it all, they found faith and life and hope and fulfilment in the Lord Jesus Christ.

It was exciting, exhilarating and challenging listening to them share the path they had trod. It was also humbling. I listened with rapt attention to the questions they asked, the experiences they had, and how the Almighty God of all creation met and answered them.

But why was I there? Why were they relating this to me?

Well, the reason I was asked to sit in was because part of what the Lord had used in their lives was the book entitled *Promises* written by the elder. And part of what the Lord had used in their lives was a series of video teaching that we had produced, also with the elder, based on the Tabernacle.

These two things were a part of their story. They formed part of what the Lord had used to bring them to Himself. God had used these to answer their questions and teach them of the Way.

They shared they were duplicating the VCD teaching series on the Tabernacle. They were giving it to people they were sharing with.

What was the question that had earlier occupied my mind? Oh, yes, '*Is it all worth it?*' Well, it was resoundingly answered by the Grace and Goodness of our Heavenly Father, 'Yes!'

He is our Father in Heaven. And He is using the video programmes. He is using us, and He is distributing the programmes in ways that we do not know of and have no way to know.

I've had the joy of seeing the faces of these two saints. And I heard them share their terribly sad story. I was humbled by their soft smiles and a light in their eyes that seems to radiate from their faces.

The power of the Good News had turned great sorrow, great grief into a profound joy, and an intense peace was made visible in their lives.

# 32

# March 2006 - Flip...Flap... Flutter

The pages of the calendar seem to fly off the wall. It gives the impression that time has consumed too much coffee. Now, instead of plodding onward, it is in the final throes of a race, closing the remaining distance in the shortest possible time.

It was just yesterday we were travelling in the east of Turkey on our second visit to the east with our friend from Izmir. We travelled to where they are now dealing with an outbreak of the Avian Flu. Our purpose was to visit isolated Christians to be an encouragement. We went to encourage them, but often it was we who were encouraged.

After that we have travelled repeatedly to Izmir. We have been filming more lessons in the series on Isaiah. They are working to create a broad curriculum of fundamental Bible teaching.

We have been filming for a year. And in the course of the year we have tried many set-ups. We have used a classroom setting and a cross-table dialogue. We have tried the classic, single person talking to camera. We have created a Turkish *Şark Köşesi*[1] and used that to film some lessons. We have been searching for the most effective means to communicate this in-depth Bible teaching.

Travelling back and forth from Istanbul each month can be difficult. But Tülin said, 'This is very rewarding and sometimes a fun time.' She added, 'I find the teaching in Isaiah very profitable for myself.'

Our Annual Sojourn in the UK

Every year we return to the UK for my annual health checks. As I've grown older, I have been diagnosed with diabetes. It is important to monitor and manage a chronic disease such as this.

So, as per my wont, we flew back to the UK. Now, it seems like it was yesterday that we were met at the airport in London. We were brought to some wonderful digs in Redbourn. The village of Redbourn is a small community neighbouring Hemel Hempstead. It is close to family and church. Nice.

But all that was long ago.

We have come to the UK for a three-month stint — and now less than one month remains. But, I hasten to add, I feel like time is screaming by. I am sure, in the blink of an eye everything that is now 'future' to me will be but a past memory.

Before we know it, we will be back in Istanbul.

But we have not been idle while in the UK. We have continued to edit and create video. We've helped our older son John and his wife Laura liquidate their home and move to Atlanta, GA, USA. We've re-packed and shipped our remaining worldly goods and memorabilia to Turkey. Lord willing, they will arrive the day after we return to Istanbul in March. I have mixed feelings about our boxes being shipped to Turkey. We have done this with no guarantee of being able to renew our residence permit. And to add a bit of spice to our lives, there is a question whether my current residence permit has enough time to run on it to import the boxes. Hmm…

In all this change, in all this turmoil, where can we find peace? How can we be content? So many questions - and questions we cannot answer.

Well, peace cannot come from our circumstances - we can hope it does but experience declares it does not happen.

But our God has declared that He is able to do abundantly above and beyond what we can ask or imagine. It is the last word '*imagine*' that intrigues me as I have a vivid imagination. Turning my eyes from what is happening, what may happen, and what the future holds, I can rest and trust and know peace by looking to God, the author and finisher of my faith.

# 33

# March 2006 - If Not Here...
## Then There

I t had to be done. And no one else could do it.

I was thankful that the bitterly cold wind that had spent the previous four days howling down the Bosphorus had been replaced by still, sunny skies. Albeit, it was still cool. But I was no longer feeling smitten by stinging arrows of ice flung from the whirlwind of northern fury. And to think, growing up in Canada, doing daily battle with the winter elements was once normal and not at all noteworthy. I guess I'm getting soft in my old age.

I gathered up what I thought would be required, descended the stairs, and turned left out the front door of our building. At the end of the street, I turned left again and up over the ridge and began the descent down the steep cobbled street. We call this the 'Post Office hill' because the Post Office is at the bottom of the hill. This makes a handy landmark for people coming to our flat, although the hill is so steep as to discourage all but the truly dedicated from making the ascent.

As I neared the bottom of the hill, I could hear the sounds of construction or, maybe more to the point, destruction. The Post Office was gone. Well, the function of the Post Office was gone. The building was still there. But it was now filled with the sounds of jack-hammers and workers bashing and thumping and carrying on the demolition of the old. This is the inevitable step that precedes reconstruction and renewal. I don't know what it will be when it is finished, but it will look very nice.

I wondered where the Post Office had gone to. Oh well, that was not where I was heading today. The task for this afternoon was far more daunting than a mere trip to the Post Office.

I turned right past the former Post Office. I stepped a bit warily as I went by, because of the crashing debris falling against the glass of the main window. At any moment I expected the glass to give way in an avalanche of glass and broken bits of masonry to pour forth. Such an event would inundate the street with and engulf any unfortunate who at that moment was crossing in front. Thankfully, now was not its chosen time to collapse, although I dare say it was not far off.

Up to the corner, and I turned into the first door on the right, up some narrow stairs, nicely finished in marble, and into the office of the *Noter*[1]. I entered a crowded, grimy little room, with cigarette smoke hanging thick in the air. The ceiling was low, and the room was full of people sitting on chairs waiting and groups of people clustered at a long, high bar-like desk. On the opposite side of the 'bar' were several ladies at computers and typewriters. They were charged with preparing a vast range of documents. In Turkey, a vast diversity of documents must be notarised to complete a transaction.

My first question: 'Where do I start?'

And coming from the UK, where queuing is second nature, I was puzzled, 'Where is the end of the queue?' And I was even questioning if there was a queue?

*What do I do?*

*Argh...* was my feeling.

I moved to the bar and waited near one lady. I saw people leave and people come. Some people moved in front of me. *I really did't know how this worked.*

Finally, a lady bellowed, 'Next in the queue.'

'Uh, what queue?' I queried. She looked disdainfully at me.

But as there wasn't a rush of people to the spot in front of her, I moved over.

She ordered her papers on her desk and did other tasks. I couldn't determine any function she was fulfilling. Finally, she turned to me.

My task was to register a power of attorney. I began holding out the sample I had brought with me. She snatched the paper from my hand, glanced at it and barked, 'Are you giving the power of attorney or the company?'

'Me...' I said hesitantly. The question seemed rather pointless to me. I stumbled and paused. But my hesitation was enough. There quickly followed a barrage of questions in abrupt succession, ending with a demand to see my ID.

Well, that did it.

A foreign passport: no, no, *no.* This would not do. I would need it translated. And by translated she meant by an official, authorised translator. This, being Turkey, meant that the translation would need to be notarised. Only when that was done, could I hope to progress further.

'Go see the lady over there,' she said, gesturing towards a rather large cluster of people. Somewhere beyond the hunched shoulders of middle-aged men, there must be somebody who could shed light on my dilemma.

My heart sank as I made my way towards the knot of men. I did not really know who it was that I was supposed to talk to. I stuffed my papers back in my pocket and slunk out the door. Down the narrow stairs to the peace and tranquillity of the street I retreated.

*Peace and tranquillity of the street?!?* Well, I would never have described it like that before I went into the Noter's office.

I turned back the way I had come and cautiously passed by the former Post Office. The rain of debris was continuously pelting down. As it clattered against the glass, I thought, 'Any time now it will explode outwards.' In the next block was yet another Noter. You know the old saying, 'If at first you don't succeed, go to a different Noter.' Or, well, something like that.

I made my way gingerly up the stairs and into a room quite similar to the previous one. There were clusters of people, chairs full of people, the sounds of fingers flying on keyboards. Mind you, there was no tobacco smoke. Most - but not all - official offices are smoke-free now. That's nice.

As in the first Noter, I didn't know where to start. I shuffled up to the desk and the lady looked up. I said what I wanted and showed her my dreaded foreign passport, gasp.

She said, 'Go talk to the lady in the corner.'

Now, I didn't know who that was. But as there were only two ladies in the corner, I had a 50-50 chance. I got it right on the second try.

She asked if I had a residence permit, to which I replied I did. She then said that I could do the power of attorney with that. With that alone, no need to get my passport officially translated and notarised.

Great!

This was very good news indeed, but this morning I didn't leave the house with my residence permit. So, thanking her, I left the office and made my way back up the very steep hill to the flat. At our building I trudged back up to the top of the building. Just in case you are wondering, we do not benefit from the modern convenience known as a lift. I picked up the residence permit and slogged back down to the Noter.

Well, my doctor told me I needed more exercise.

Now I knew where to start. I went back to the lady who had told me the residence permit was sufficient. She took my papers and told me to sit down. I would have gladly sat down had there been any empty chairs. So, I leaned against the wall. There I began the main occupation of people in a Noter's office — waiting.

And I had ample opportunity to practise the art of waiting. After a while, a chair became free, so that eased the task somewhat.

I mused that I should have brought a book. In the time I was waiting, I could have written a book. Not really, but it is what I thought.

In the end the crowds lessened and then the lady held out my papers. My first reaction was, 'When did she do my paperwork?' Then she told me to go to another lady behind the desk. This lady would now start my task. My task was far from being finished. It was just now beginning.

I had a sample power of attorney that needed just one change and a date. She looked at it — it was a rather long document. Then she took a pair of scissors and cut the offending date out. She then photocopied the page, put the photocopied page in a typewriter, and typed in the new date.

Much faster and easier than retyping the whole thing.

With the correct date filled in, I was off to the Notary Public himself. Of course, there was the mandatory bit of waiting to do first. He signed the front, turned the paper over, and read the text. Then he asked to see my ID. He knew enough to know that Richard is more often than not abbreviated from the long to the short form. I was given only the short form of my name at birth, so my short form given name was accepted.

With that confirmed, he signed again and gave me the papers. Off I went to the lady I started with. She did something or other, then sent me to the last lady. That was where I paid the fee.

Half a day, and one aspect of trying to import our boxes of keep-sakes into the country done. Done, and yet the task was barely begun.

Next week promises to be equally exciting. Monday, we are off to the main police building in Istanbul. There we begin the process of applying for an extension of our residence permits. And then I need to take the power of attorney, done today, to the agent who is importing our boxes.

Things change and activities come and go. Our local Post Office moves — but the function of the Post Office carries on somewhere. Things and tasks have to be done. Some jobs are pleasant and some are not. But in it all, and through it all, and in spite of it all, our God remains our faithful and solid rock. Come what may, all changes notwithstanding, He is our solace, our source and shield in all we do.

# 34

# April 2006 - Computers Make Life Easier

W e were setting up to shoot a series of Bible studies in Istanbul.

A blue screen[1] was hoisted to its full height, and falling like a blue wave to the floor. I had set the lights and, after a few adjustments, they seemed to be set right. Our speaker had been collected from the airport the previous day and today was to be the first day of a four-day shoot. We had planned a series on Spiritual Warfare from Ephesians and a two-part series on Servanthood from Timothy. Finally, two special programmes (for use with Turks in Germany): one about Christmas and the other about Easter.

Our living room was thrown into disarray to become our makeshift 'studio'. We shifted the furniture out of the way and hung jet black curtains on the window to exclude the powerful spring sunshine. I took a monitor off my video editing suite so it could do its duty as part of our 'teleprompter'.

A teleprompter is a marvellous innovation and we created our own home-made version. We fitted a two-way mirror in front of the camera. The monitor below the mirror reflected the notes onto the mirror and so, the speaker could read his notes while at the same time looking directly at the camera. This was easier for the speaker as many people find staring at a 'one-eyed monster' difficult. The result was that he was always looking directly at the camera.

*Our home-made teleprompter*

The speaker had spent time in prayer and reviewing his notes. All the equipment was ready. The last thing was to bring our trusty laptop out to the 'studio'. All we had to do was hook it up to the monitor that was part of the teleprompter and we were ready to shoot.

At first the problems presented a curiosity. Words like 'why the…' and 'what the…' stumbled across my lips. The laptop seemed testy, I would go as far to say it was even uncooperative. Things it would normally do with a 'click' *it wasn't doing*. Things it would do 'automatically' it was refusing to do.

What do you do when a computer misbehaves? You re-boot it. You may feel like 'kicking' it, but, no, you 're-boot' it. It is almost a mantra - problem with your computer, turn it off and back on again. This action has fixed a myriad of problems, a panacea for most things Windows.

So I turned it off.

I turned it back on.

However, it failed to turn back on. Well, the screen came alive, the electricity was flowing, but almost immediately up came an error message. Now this was a new error message and an error message I had never seen before. And that was as far as the computer would go. This was an error message before the dreaded Windows 'Blue Screen of Death'[2]. But it never got that far. It was a black screen (not blue) - and an error message. That was it.

This was new. And this was uncharted territory. This was scary. With known problems you may have a raft of things to try — but this was brand new... *what to do?*

There it sat. There I sat. I was staring at the screen... the words of the error message staring back at me. To say I was speechless was an understatement. I hadn't expected this. This had never happened to me before. There we sat, my laptop and I.

We were ready to shoot. Our Turkish speaker had travelled from Germany where he was based. He had made a special trip for this shoot. He was prepared. The room was readied. The blue screen (for video) was set. The lights were set. The camera was primed and ready to shoot. But the teleprompter can only work with a computer. Simple really, no computer, no teleprompter. And it follows, no teleprompter, no shoot, and no shoot, no programme. If there was no programme, then no encouragement for the saints. This was not an inconvenience, this was serious.

Now I don't know a lot about computers, but what I know, I tried. I am inclined to be - hmm, what is a kind word for 'stubborn like a mule'? Maybe it would be, er, 'steadfast'? Okay, I steadfastly tried to restart the computer. Again and again, and over and over, I turned it off and back on again — waiting between the off and on attempts. But it was determined not to respond to my machinations. And respond it did not do.

Whatever I tried, it returned the same response. Consistently, it fell at the first hurdle and refused to alter its chosen course. Well, I gave it full credit for consistency. For it was steadfast in its refusal to move beyond that first error message.

In my, uh, steadfastness, I tried every variation on a theme to coax the laptop back into a semblance of health. Alas, to no avail.

The laptop would not be cajoled into compliance.

Clearly, if Plan 'A' fails, you turn to Plan 'B'. We must go to Plan 'B' - er, **what is Plan 'B'?**

The only Plan 'B' that came to mind involved dragging the PC out of my office. We could hook it up and then, at last, get down to the real work.

Great, wonderful, a way forward, light at the end of the tunnel, a solution...

**Except that the PC was ill.**

When we returned from the UK, a hard drive had failed in the PC. This was not a storage drive or an additional drive. Oh, no, this was the main hard drive which had failed. So, earlier, I fitted a new hard drive. I had re-installed Windows and got everything **nearly** back and **nearly** working.

This is a happy story so far, isn't it?

But **before** I got it 100% working, the new hard drive began to fail. Error message upon error message came up. There were faults upon faults. All were cascading together into an avalanche of ill tidings. I threw Norton System Works at it. It found and repaired problem after problem after problem. Sadly, every time I ran it, it found more problems. The drive was ill. It was very ill. However, it was still working - just.

So, we installed the teleprompter software on our ill PC. We could only do this because of what Tülin did that very morning. In a fit of responsibility and resourcefulness, she had copied the software off the now immobile and uncooperative laptop. She had safely squirrelled it away, little realising that in a few hours that one act would be key to Plan 'B'. We moved the PC and got it all set up. It was working and ready to go. Hey, that was not bad. We wanted to shoot in the morning, and **by early evening** we were ready to go.

Once working, that evening we shot two messages. The adage, 'make hay while the sun shines' came to mind but in this case, 'shoot video while the computer is still working'.

So, over the remaining days, we continued shooting our planned series of videos. And when I was not doing that, I tried to prod the laptop back to life. Oh, and the never-ending task of loading video tape onto the editing suite. Once on the edit suite, we would check to ensure that what we shot was good. It was a bit of a three-ring circus. I was trying to be in two places at the same time and keep three or four tasks going at the same time.

Whilst amid this somewhat frenetic activity, one of my wisdom teeth decided, *in its wisdom*, to rear its ugly head. It forcefully announced its presence in my mouth. Now I'm too old for wisdom teeth creating problems. I stayed up late trying to sort out the laptop. I was not getting much sleep courtesy of my wisdom tooth and, oh, the shoot was going on.

Well, the laptop, finally, hmm, let me say, was 'working' again but after a fashion. It was doing bizarre and unexpected things. Well, I guess an old dog can learn new tricks. Mind you, some tricks it learned were really weird. It remained not only very ill, but, I feared, terminally ill. The solution to its ailment would involve having to copy all the data from the hard drive. Once that was done, we would wipe it clean and reinstall Windows from scratch. And once working again, bring it up-to-date and reload all the programmes. Oh, yes, and bring the programmes up-to-date as well. Ohh, I feel worn out describing it all. All in all, there was probably two or three days' worth of work in order just to 'get to work'.

As a friend recently wrote regarding the saga of my laptop - my digital servant:

'Your servant is in bed, ill and terribly tormented. I can only have compassion for you, not your servant. Just as one must never get angry at an inanimate object, it stands to reason one must not pity it either. I am afraid it is hard to expect miracles for this soulless servant of yours. It can neither be damned nor blessed. We can only put it into order or chaos.'

Well, to put it into 'order' I need two or three days. I don't know when I will find those days.

The shoot was done. The programmes were in the bag, or in this case on tape. They were loaded on the computer and were ready for editing.

On Monday we leave for Adana in the south. From thence we will travel over to Antakya (Antioch), Urfa, Diyarbakir, Midyat and Mardin. The main reason for the trip is to meet the saints in Diyarbakir. There we will discuss a video project we are doing with them. Secondarily, we will meet isolated saints and try to encourage them.

Lord willing, we will be back in Istanbul for Easter. Then we will go down to Izmir (Smyrna) for a fortnight. This is so we can continue the shoot on the Isaiah series to support the work there.

I feel worn out by it all and we have just begun.

The new series we have just shot is entitled 'Spiritual Warfare'. Well, sometimes it can be a struggle, a battle, to get even simple things done. But we can rest in knowing the battle is not ours but His. Even if we feel the struggle and have to deal with the aftermath.

# 35

# April 2006 - In Search of a Good Restaurant

I was not in control - I was there by force of events and we were waiting for a nondescript white van to arrive.

This act of waiting was performed in the '*Söz Kitap Evi*' or, in English, 'The Word Book Store'. It is a Christian bookstore in the city of Adana, in south-east Turkey.

Adana sprawls in the shadow of the mighty *Toros*[1] mountain range. Long has there been a city perched on the banks of the Seyhan River amid the fertile Çukurova plain.

The story of Adana stretches from a mound in the centre of the city called the *Tepebağ* tumulus. This has been dated to 6,000 BC. The city has passed through Hittite, Egyptian, Greek, Roman, Armenian, Byzantine, Ottoman and now it is a vibrant part of Turkey.

Back in the early 1980s, there was no church in the city. Well, that is not 100% accurate, there was a Roman Catholic church. I guess what I mean is, there were no other churches and certainly no Protestant church in the city.

There were a few young men who gathered together in a home to hear the Word of God shared, study the Bible, sing a few hymns, and pray. There was certainly **no** Christian book store. Then, the population of the city was about one million souls.

But, now in 2006, we were standing in a Christian book store speaking with the leaders of two different Turkish churches in this city. The city now boasts a population of roughly two million. I know nothing stays the same, but I am amazed at how things have changed.

The nondescript white van arrived. We — the leaders of the two churches, some visiting brothers and our travelling companions — departed the bookstore and piled in. We were off to break bread together.

Tülin and I had arrived just an hour earlier and she remained at the home of one elder in the church. I had been commandeered to attend this impromptu meeting.

It was good that we were going for a meal, as my diabetes means I need little fill-ups throughout the day. The good old days of going about one's business and grabbing a bite to eat **whenever** had passed. It had well and truly faded into the distant past.

Now, back in Adana, I looked right and left and my, oh my, how things had changed. I recognised many landmarks, boulevards and buildings, but I was confronted with many, many new things.

Well, when I say 'new', I mean they were not there when we lived in Adana. Buildings had been built since then and become tired and worn. But there were also new, 'new buildings' adorning the city like a stunning garland. I was blown away by the fruits of the architects' skill. This was not a cookie-cutter approach; each building had their own unique flourishes. And some offered a liberal splash of flamboyance.

The driver of the van aggressively weaved in and out of traffic. He was following roads I had travelled in the past. But then he turned abruptly and crossed the Seyhan River on a bridge. There was no 'bridge' there in my time… Now there was and it looked like it had been there, well, forever.

Once across the bridge, we were in a simpler part of town. Here there were no high-rises, as we had left all vestiges of the new Adana behind us. This was more like the 'old' Adana that we knew so well. There was a profusion of dumpy looking two-storey structures. Each was slap-bang up against its neighbour. We were surrounded by an assortment of unkempt, paint peeling structures. Now when I say 'paint peeling' that only applied to where there had once been paint. Indeed, my first impression would have been 'run down', but I'm not 100% certain that even when they were first built, they looked significantly different. Often, buildings of this, er, style, were never actually 'finished'.

I heard we were going to a 'good' restaurant. That was good - I like 'good' restaurants. But the area of town we were now slowly making our way through was – er, well, more rustic. It didn't bode well for finding a 'good' restaurant. Now let the reader understand what I mean by 'good'. A 'good' restaurant will be 'safe', as well as 'tasting good' and 'reasonably priced'.

The van slowed and then suddenly swerved to the curb and lurched to a halt. Everyone started tumbling out as, evidently, we had arrived. But where exactly had we arrived?

I scanned up and down the grubby street. The dust was hanging in the air. My eye was drawn to the litter as it lay abandoned on the floor. The occasional breath of wind would give the garbage wings. I could not pick out anything I would describe as a 'good' restaurant. Gazing up the road, I saw a typical small, crowded town scene. Lorries, cars, other vehicles, and people clogged the road. There were bicycles and motorcycles and, oh, the odd horse cart just to keep it interesting. The whole scene that confronted me had a forlorn sense of general neglect. It looked like no one really cared or ever had cared. Here we were in the heat and humidity, walking in an area with a depressing feeling of neglect and abandonment.

My eyes continued darting left and right, but for the life of me I couldn't spot a 'good' restaurant anywhere. We walked down the broken and uneven footpath. Then, without warning, we turned into a shabby building. This, ah, place was, um, rather 'simple'.

The 'dining area' was not very large - I said 'simple'. Many helping hands moved tables until we had space for all eight of us. Once our tables were assembled, we dominated the restaurant.

I'm not sure that we had the benefit of a 'menu'. It was more a 'What do you have?' kind of establishment. They would tell you what they had and, according to that, you would order. It was decided rather quickly that one of us would have lamb chops. The rest of us chose 'Adana Kebab' as our main course.

Adana Kebab is the hallmark of, well, Adana. It is a special kebab claimed by and named after the city. It is made of minced lamb and spices, kneaded by hand. Then it is formed on to a flat skewer and cooked over a charcoal-fired brazier. It comes in two varieties, 'normal' and 'spicy'. To my palate the spicy variety is too hot for me. It is hot to my tongue… lips… eyes…ears… throat… Let's just say, it is for those who love to burn… and perspire… and cry…

Once the tables were set and the order given, there was a buzz of activity. First to come were *meze* or appetisers. Turks are famous for the variety of their appetisers, and in this restaurant come they did, in rapid succession.

First was a piping hot mini-Turkish pizza-like dish fresh from the oven. These little pizza-like *meze* are round with a leavened pizza-like crust. The topping comprises mince with a red pepper sauce. Mind you, it is light on the mince, often it is more a dusting of mince. Oh, and no cheese or tomato sauce. I said, *'pizza-like'*, meaning more shape and base than any other similarities.

These had come forth from a large oven that is part of the restaurant. When I say oven, what comes to your mind? I would not be surprised if you said something shiny and modern. Maybe something electric or gas-powered comes to mind. Well, a Turkish baker's oven is a dome-shaped brick structure. It is large and dominates the wall in which it is situated. There is a chimney, as it is heated by a wood fire set ***inside the oven.*** There is a small opening where the wood is passed into the fire. And through the same opening the things to be baked are passed in and out. There is no door to contain the heat or inhibit the loading and unloading of the oven. In winter, it is a cosy place to work. In summer, it is like tending the fires of hell.

A whole variety of dough-based dishes are prepared on site. They are cooked and presented fresh to the diners.

There is an art to operating an oven such as this. The dough-based products are hand prepared. Things like the mini-Turkish-pizzas or bread, which is formed into loaf-like shapes, are prepared in front of the oven. The bread is a bloomer style loaf, no pans are used. Once prepared, the baker takes these items and puts them on a wooden paddle. This paddle has a long handle, two-and-a-half metres plus.

There is a real skill in being able to feed the oven with such a long wooden paddle. The further your hands are from the paddle end, the heavier and more ungainly the paddle becomes. The baker starts by loading the paddle with the things to be baked. His hands are near the paddle end. But as he swings it around and then plunges it into the belly of the furnace, it becomes much harder.

Once he gets the paddle past the narrow aperture, he must place the items in just the right spot. At his chosen spot, he deposits the items to bake. He must carefully choose the location, for if it is too close to the fire, it will bake too quickly. And again, if too far away, it will not bake quickly enough. Oh, and to complicate things, the oven is rarely empty. He must find an appropriate empty place to lay the new items amongst the currently baking items.

Turks make a special bread called *pide*[2]. This is made from normal leavened dough. The difference is in the form, as it is not formed like a bloomer loaf, but it is spread out relatively flat. The baker flattens and stretches the dough. Sometimes the *pide* is an exaggerated oval — oval, but stretched out longer. It has a rectangular shape with rounded corners. He works the dough using his fingers, pushing the dough out and down. Thus he creates a distinctive look to the bread. His fingers make a series of wee bumps and valleys – like ridges and furrows in a ploughed field. Then he tops the bread with sprinkles of sesame seeds and black cumin seeds. Thusly prepared, it too, is 'paddled' into the oven to bake.

The baker stands steadfast in front of the oven. This is his place in the restaurant. The intense heat emanating out of the oven does not distract him. He is perspiring profusely but keeps a sharp eye on the items in the oven. When the time is right, in flies the paddle. He deftly slips it under the freshly cooked bread or mini-pizzas or whatever it is and draws it out.

This is truly 'fresh from the oven' bread. As the freshly baked goods come forth from the oven, the restaurant is filled with the fragrance. It is brought to the table piping hot. To accompany the bread, the waiters bring soft cheese, fresh butter and onions.

You could be tempted to make a feast of the bread alone! It is profoundly appetising.

But no, this was but the beginning. After the bread dishes, with their cheese, butter and onions, flowed a procession of salads.

One of my favourite *meze* is humus, dressed with lemon juice and fresh olive oil. Often the sides of the dish are dressed with pieces of pickle and quartered tomatoes. The humus goes with the *pide* bread like hand and glove. Wonderful.

Then *cacık*[3] – a yogurt and cucumber dish arrived. Cucumbers are shredded and mixed with fresh yogurt garnished with mint and garlic.

A dish we never had when we lived in Adana in the early 80s was *babaganuş*[4]. This dish is made from aubergine roasted over hot coals. It is pureed and mixed with red peppers and, yes, olive oil.

I could have easily eaten my fill of these salads and *mezes*. I would have been happy - content, even. Well, maybe even to the point of overindulging.

There was olive oil on the table to dress the salads. But then the waiters brought some plastic bottles filled with a red liquid. They had refilled these ubiquitous plastic water bottles with the dark red liquid. This is called *nar ekşisi*[5] in Turkish. This is a special sauce in this region and is a common dressing for salads.

Real *nar ekşisi* is made in the village. The ladies take fresh pomegranates and extract the seeds. These are then squeezed. The resultant mash is boiled and strained. The boiling is done until it is reduced to a thick syrup. This thick liquid is then poured into the former water bottles.

Holes had been roughly punched in the lids of the erstwhile water bottles. So now, according to your taste, you could squeeze some *nar ekşisi* onto your salad. It was fantastic. It added a subtle and yet appealing flavour to the salad. The *nar ekşisi* is both tart and sweet at the same time. Hence it was a wonderful, complementary accent for many of the salads.

Let's look at the salads.

Another of my favourites is a walnut salad. I smiled when it arrived on our table. It is also called a *gavurdağ salatası* - or Infidel Mountain Salad. It is made from crushed walnuts, finely chopped tomatoes, onions, chopped peppers and *nar ekşisi*. If it is not too spicy, it is wonderful. I love walnuts.

There was an onion salad where the onions were lightly cooked. And another onion salad comprising raw onions and sumac. Sumac is made of the drupes of Rhus coriaria. They are ground into a reddish-purple powder and used as a spice in Middle Eastern cuisine. It adds a tart, lemony taste to salads or meat. Hence, although before me was an onion salad, it had a slightly lemon-like taste.

Another salad was made with red cabbage, cucumber, tomatoes and onions. The ingredients were all shredded and stirred together. It was dressed with lemon juice and olive oil on top.

And there was, as standard fare, a mixed salad. This is a salad of tomatoes, cucumbers, onions chopped into fairly small pieces and mixed. It is topped with salt and lemon juice and olive oil.

Finally, the last salad was a special one made from pureed tomatoes. The chef cut the tomatoes in half, scooped out and discarded the seeds. The tomatoes were finely chopped. To this, they add finely chopped onions, peppers, chillies and cucumber. It tasted great.

The salads alone presented a rich variety that tickled the taste buds. They alone assuage that gnawing hunger. And all this was well before the main course. As they say, they saved the best till last.

Our Adana kebab arrived, steaming hot from the brazier. By this time, the edge had been totally removed from our hunger. Now, we could leisurely enjoy the grilled meat. As the fancy took us, we could add whatever salad we felt would complement the flavour. We were free to add a little onion, a little mixed salad, a little cabbage. Hence, every mouthful could be tailor-made to suit the moment.

It was there in this relaxed atmosphere that I looked at our little group. Several conversations were going on. I noted we were a mixed bag - different foreigners and Turks. Some people were living in Adana and others in other parts of Turkey.

But the question remains, 'What brought these different people together?' What gave us the wonderful time around the table? Many of us had only just met.

We were all united in our love for the Lord, who has redeemed us and placed us in His Body. And we were united in our love for the Turkish people.

In the end, it was indeed a 'good' restaurant.

# 36

# April 2006 - Dark, Wet and Blind

O ur journey through the east of Turkey was not a touristic endeavour. We did not go to see the sights - but to see people. Our travelling companion knew all these people in the various locations. Now we had arrived in Antakya and there were several people he wanted to visit.

Evening arrived and it was time for us to go. As we, our travelling companion, our hosts and ourselves, put our shoes on to leave, my ears were filled with the sound of falling rain. It sounded torrential. Normally it wouldn't be a problem. But on this trip, I did not bring my winter coat. For clarity, my waterproof winter coat. More than that, my waterproof winter coat with a waterproof hat safely secreted in an inner pocket. Now that would have worked fine. But I didn't bring it.

So I stood outside the car in my suit jacket with the rain falling.

We set out in the car despite our destination not being far, but it was too far to walk in the rain. In more conducive weather, it would have been a pleasant stroll. It was early evening with little street lighting. It was raining. And we weren't 100% sure where the location of the home we were going to was. When we arrived, or thought we had arrived, the path to our destination was in the dark.

We piled out of the car and stood in the gloom. We puzzled which way to go - which meant we were standing in the rain. A passer-by kindly helped us and, armed with their directions, we stepped off the road and into the dark. It was a nondescript path leading down off the road and along a rather steep bank. Proceeding cautiously, the rain was less a concern than where to put our feet. The dirt-stone path came to some concrete steps. There was still insufficient light to know where to put our feet. The concrete steps were of the home-made variety. Let the reader understand - of differing heights. This type of stairs is always a challenge and more so in the dark. Oh, and there was no railing to guide and assist in the descent.

After the, uh, stair-like construction, we proceeded down the dirt path and the shadowy form of a house coalesced out of the murk. We had phoned ahead to say we were coming, but the gate was cloaked in darkness. We rang the bell. Well, not a bell actually. It made the sound of a bird twittering. The sound was not near. It was away in the distance. The rain continued its relentless onslaught as we stood in a clutch around the locked gate.

Again the door 'bird' was pushed and the twittering sounded our presence once again. Still no light and still no action, and the rain continued to fall. I was feeling like a rat being slowly drowned.

It was on the fourth or fifth sounding of the bird that a light flick-ered into life. Down the way, a figure came out of a door and began making their way towards the gate.

The house comprised three rooms in a row. The door was in the middle room. From thence you could either go to the right, which was the kitchen and toilet, or to the left, which was the bedroom.

A lady of an age I would guess at something between 45 to 50 warmly greeted us and conducted us down the path to the door. We popped our shoes off at the door and entered a simple whitewashed concrete room. In the centre of the room there was a wood stove radiating heat like a mini-sun. Truly, it was too hot, and yet it felt like a welcome blast of heat. The drying process began. Ill prepared as I was, I needed drying out.

The man of the house was standing and we were greeting him and he us. We had been told he had lost his sight. So, although his eyes were open, and he was 'looking', he wasn't 'seeing'. I reached out and bumped his hand, so he would know that I was ready to shake hands.

Then, after warm greetings all round, we sat down. Our travelling companion was outgoing. He sat beside our host and chatted with him in an animated conversation covering a range of topics.

As I was sitting a few feet away and he couldn't see, it was as if I wasn't there. No eye contact - no sound equals not being there. He who speaks not, is not.

The initial blast of heat from the stove subsided and the lady of the house loaded some more wood into the mouth of the beast. It was slow in building up heat, which made sitting comfortable but slowed down my drying out.

In the end, it was a pleasant visit, even for the one who was quiet and so not there - uh, that would be me. But when visiting with a blind man, I needed to break the habit of a lifetime to let my presence be known. And when I speak, I need to smile with my face for it to be conveyed in my speech.

The purpose of our travels was to meet and encourage people. For us, it was a small thing to go out on a dark evening in the rain.

We trust they were encouraged. As their burning stove warmed and dried us, so we hoped our conversation warmed and encouraged them.

# 37

# April 2006 - Ah, the City of Urfa - Ancient Edessa

Travelling with our friend from Izmir, we carried on from Adana to Urfa. He used to live in the east and was now making annual trips *'out east'* to visit the folks he knows. This was our second trip accompanying him on his journeys. For us, this was a real treat as he organised and knew where he was going. For me, being a shy person, this took the edge off of going somewhere 'new'.

The further east you go, the further you are from western influences. And, to a degree, you travel back in time. You certainly encounter a different culture. On this day we travelled to the city of Urfa - or its full name, Şanlıurfa[1] (Glorious Urfa[2]). This city is just up the plain from the ruins of ancient Harran - from whence came Abraham.

Urfa[3], known as Edessa in the long past, was once a great Christian city. It was on the border of the Roman Empire with the Persians. Hence, there was always some conflict and war nearby. That makes for a rocky history. Now there are very few Christians left in this city.

Normally we stayed with people in the places we visited. However, in Urfa this was not possible. Our host had arranged for us to stay in a local B&B, but this was a B&B with a difference, a B&B Turkish style.

*Our lodgings for the night...*

We pulled up in an older part of town and stopped in a small parking area. We climbed out of the car and made our way back to a stone building.

Our accommodations would be in this Turkish *Han*. A *han* was once the **Travelodge** of the Ottoman Empire. When travelling by foot, horse or camel, you needed a place to rest for the night. And the place needed to accommodate your pack animals. And as caravans were transporting valuable goods — a *han* needed to be secure. Hence the powerful stone walls and single point of access that is typical of these way stations. These stone-built *hans* stretched over the empire along the major trade routes. Ours was a small *han* - but stone-built and filled with Ottoman fixtures and fittings. You might say, either we were travelling in time, or staying in a living museum.

We entered the *han* by descending several steps and then stepped through the thick wall and into the inner doorway. This led us into a stone-paved courtyard with rooms on both the ground and first floor level. This was a guest-house-cum-restaurant. Or was it a restaurant with rooms? I don't know, it was a bit of a mixed bag.

Immediately on one's right on entering the courtyard was a small basin with a tap. It was carved intricately in white stone, with a roof-like stone structure over it.

Beside it was a well and rope winding mechanism. These were set into the wall with an intricately carved arch and stone flowers on the wall above the arch. The old carvings in stone were a delight to look at. They had also endured, despite the years of sun and weather thrown at them.

Turkish music was drifting through the air to greet us. There were several men dressed in spotless white shirts and ties and black trousers. Some were without shoes and their trousers were rolled up at the ankles. It seems they had been washing down the *han* for some hours. As this was our first visit, we did not know if this was their daily cleaning or if this was a special 'deep clean'? The scrubbing sounds continued to 15:00.

*The interior courtyard - with fountain*

The building was built entirely of white stone, although it had become somewhat yellowed in places over the years. A Turkish *han* reflects an ancient tradition and there was much to see.

In the central courtyard there were two mature orange trees laden with luscious looking oranges. There were alcoves with cushions in which to sit and drink Turkish tea. Tucked away under the stairs was a cupboard where pigeons were raised. In the centre of the courtyard there stands a fountain. It was an eight-sided stone fountain. In the middle of the pool it had a central carved pillar from where the water sprayed. The pool surrounding it was perhaps a metre in depth. The sides were topped with large stones which were flat.

On the far wall, as one entered, were a few stairs leading up to an intricately carved two metre high decorated surround. In this surround, set on the wall, there was a basin and tap. All this was made of white stone. From there, the stairs, one to the left and one to the right, led to the first floor on opposing wings. In the courtyard, on the left, were arches and an overhang in front of the rooms on ground level. And on the first floor level there were arches (the centre one was very ornate), creating a covered walkway leading to the *sark odası* rooms. A *sark odası*[4] is a special Ottoman sitting room.

On the right of the courtyard was the highest level. It had rooms on the first floor and was topped with an open terrace with tables and chairs. There the guests could enjoy the cool of the evening in the summer, late spring and early autumn. Above the entry to the *han* there were also tables and a covered area. This made an additional outside 'sitting room', with couches on the same level as the *sark odası* rooms.

Also on the right side of the courtyard, there were two low sets of steps. They came from the right and left-hand sides and met before the great ornate doorway *(perhaps a formal restaurant)*. About half a floor below the courtyard level, there were still more rooms - a kitchen, perhaps - *well, the food must be cooked somewhere.*

The first question to be decided was did we want a room at court-yard level or first floor level. As we had never stayed there or in a similar place, we did not know what to choose. What were the pluses or minuses of being up or down? So, we asked the man which he would suggest.

'First floor,' was his quick reply. And so, our choice was made.

He grabbed our bags and made for the stone steps. This was a welcome relief for me. My tennis elbow was making strident complaints about lugging the luggage. The stone steps were set at a rather generous rise. It is amazing what a difference in the height of a stair can make. It reminded again of the passing years. My knees clearly objected to the added stretch.

We arrived at the first floor and the stone steps opened onto a stone veranda. There were columns, arches, and a metal railing. The first floor veranda went down one side, across the front wall. Then it continued up some stairs to the terrace with a stone balustrade over the rooms on the opposite side. On both sides of the courtyard, opening off the veranda, were double wooden doors. These gave access to individual rooms, the *sark odası*.

The man opened the door to 'our room'. I slipped my shoes off at the door and stepped through. The stone walls were wide. So, I entered the door, but travelled a half metre before I came into the room. There I was treated to a room decorated in the Ottoman style of a hundred plus years ago.

But the thing that caught my eye most was the fact that in the centre of the room was a low Ottoman dining room setting for eight. This was a low table on the floor and people sit on the floor around the table.

*The way the rooms were set*

'Okay,' I thought, 'but we weren't planning to eat.' Besides, there are only two of us, and, er, where do we sleep...

Our guide explained to my barrage of questions that he would remove the place settings and the tables. Then he would lay some traditional cotton filled mattresses on the floor in a bed shape. To complete the ensemble, he would add a duvet and, presto, you would have an instant bedroom. Therefore, the space could be a restaurant or a room to stay — a double duty room.

The floor was covered with individual carpets. The outer walls had five wooden cabinets set into the stone walls, three in the wall on the left, and two on the wall directly in front of us. There was a large arch inset on one wall on the left. And there were two arch insets on the wall opposite the door. These arch insets stored bedding, cushions, pillows and other things. There were three long windows in the same wall as the door — all were facing the private courtyard. The ceiling comprised a high dome decorated at its apex, a simple blue floral design. We were told this was the original decoration. Indeed, the white background was now a decidedly dirty grey.

That was the good news. The bad news, or the 'not what I was hoping for' news was there was no en suite. The toilets were down on the main level, just off the central courtyard. And they were the communal facilities for the establishment. No shower. But more to the point for my travelling frame of mind, no *alafranga* (European style loo). We were in the east, and they had the *alaturka* (eastern style squat toilet) downstairs.

This had all been arranged for us. The chap who had arranged it was standing there with us. It seemed to me to be most appropriate to receive with thanksgiving that which was offered. We said it was fine and took it.

There was more bad news coming. The price took me by surprise — it was nearly three times more expensive that I was expecting.

Ouch!

Our friend who had made the arrangements left and we settled into our *sark odası*.

As we were sitting there in our room, we could hear Turkish music mixed with the sounds of men working and talking. Now and then we could hear the sounds of plates rattling in the kitchen - *somewhere*. We felt enveloped with a feeling of relaxation, of life going on but gently passing us by.

Outside the *han* the air was filled with the sound of cars, motorcycles, a few trucks driving by. This was interspersed with the loud, insistent sound of the call to prayer every few hours. Nevertheless, my overall feeling was that there no hurry in life here in Urfa[5].

So, on our first night in Şanlıurfa, we bedded down in traditional Ottoman style in a stone-built house. What a treat. Too bad about the loo and shower.

The next morning we were to be on our own, with our hosts and travelling companion being otherwise engaged. There were no activities planned until the afternoon. Needless to say, we were feeling the need to stay still and rest. The staff of the *han* came and after some fits and starts, moved us to the room next door.

It too was set for about six people to eat - which they would change. But more to the point, **there was an en suite shower and alafranga**. Heaven. Bliss. Ahhhhh…You do not appreciate these simple things of life - until you have to do without.

Our new room… was square and as is typical, the floor was covered with carpets. The carpets in this room looked like corridor runners in a Turkish-carpet style. The previous room we were in had large rectangular Turkish carpets covering the entire floor. Around the wall at floor level were backrests - very firm, with a Turkish *kilim*[6] (rug) cover on them. One was able to sit on the floor on a stiff mattress, leaning on the wall for back support.

But we're not so eastern or accustomed to sitting thusly. The hotel workers set up a table and chairs for us to eat at and to sit on when the floor got uncomfortable. The bed, again, was a hard mattress laid on the floor.

Each room had a high arch in one wall with the base about one metre off the floor. It was here the mattresses were stored in that shelf-like alcove. The room had several alcoves with wood and glass doors - sort of like china cabinets, in blonde wood, and had lovely copper pieces or pottery gracing the shelves. The ceiling had very old Ottoman designs painted on it - flowers with curvy lines in blue and brown. The design appeared to be very old, and the white, again, was now grey, with cracks and patches here and there. Above the high walls there was first a concave section with painted designs. Then there was a convex section, again with painted designs but different. Finally, in this room, there was a slightly rectangular 'dome' with straight (neither convex nor concave) sides. In the place of a dome, there was a flat ceiling with a metre plus wide blue 'flower' painted in the centre.

Outside, above the entry in the terrace area, the 'sitting room' had an oval-shaped dome, again painted as the others. They must have been exquisite when new, as they were still beautiful, even greyed with age as they were now.

I went to the sink and washed my hands - the water was hot, so hot I had to adjust it down. Great.

Tülin and I sat that morning in large over-stuffed chairs that were brought in for us. We gazed out through the double door at the courtyard, the orange trees, and rooms on the opposite wing. The sun was gently shining down, caressing the vista before us. There were birds singing in the background, mixing with the pigeons cooing, as they perched under the arches. A refreshing and appreciated needed break.

Rarely can you enter a lost way of life. Staying these days in a *han*, especially for someone like me who loves 'old stones', was a real treat. We were not expecting a *han* experience. We were expecting, like our previous visit, roughing it on the floor and trying to ration the water, as there was not enough for all. This time, staying in a *han*, we could explore the old city at leisure.

Nice.

# 38

# April 2006 - It Was - But It Isn't - And Yet There Is

There is no formal church building in Urfa[1] - well, actually there is. Tülin and I, as two foreigners wandering the streets, were observed. Turks are both hospitable and helpful. One chap asked us if we were looking for the '***church***'. Well, once he asked his question, *we were (now) looking for the church.* He gave us directions to go down a warren of narrow alleyways. To the best of our ability, we followed his directions until we came upon a building that we recognised as church architecture.

In we went and began looking about this building, which is now an art and culture centre. Concerts and such are held there and funnily enough, the main room where Christians once gathered is still filled with benches - like pews. We asked the man who works there what it was and he said it was a cultural centre. We asked what it was '***before***', he said a factory. Pressing on, we asked what it was prior to that and he admitted it had been a Syrian Orthodox Church. He may as well have stated it earlier - the architecture declared its roots. But he said that all the Christians left. He didn't say when and he didn't say why. But the building had been converted into an art and culture centre.

He didn't know of the few believers still in Urfa. And since there is no official building for them to gather in, they gather in homes.

*Former Syrian Orthodox Church building*

We had been invited to join them for their mid-week meeting.

They arrived in drips and drabs. The first to arrive was a family with children. When I say 'with children' I mean they had a veritable tribe of children. Their children kept coming and coming to the point I had difficulty keeping count. There were lots. Other folk came in and soon the sitting room was filled. All but one, I believe, were followers of Christ.

They were a mixed group, including a Turk from Boston with impeccable English. Then there was the chap who had been attacked by a group with knives. And at a different time, by a gang with clubs. His business, a tea shop, was situated under a 2.5 tonne water tank. Well, it was there, until it was wiped out when the tank collapsed and crushed the shop. No one was seriously injured, but the tables and chairs were pressed flat.

In this small gathering, each one had their own story. Invariably, the stories were of hardship and difficulty, pain and suffering. We sang a few Christian songs and then came the sharing from the Bible.

After the sharing, the chap who I think was not a believer excused himself and left. At the end of it all, the speaker suggested we pray.

Now I had an expectation of the time of prayer. I thought several might pray and that would be it.

But not as I expected, each one prayed. But what I didn't expect was they kept on praying. The prayers were not long, nor were the prayers eloquent. They were not speaking in finely composed Turkish prose. The prayers were from the heart. The prayers were genuine. They prayed for each other. They prayed with heartfelt, spontaneous prayer, one for another.

They even prayed for the quiet foreign guy in the corner. They didn't take time to share their needs - they knew them. With simple prayers they brought the needs of each other to the Lord. Over all there was a sense of broken-ness. This was a real prayer meeting.

Afterwards, in the small discussions, one chap drew attention to me. He said, *'I don't know this brother's name. I don't know whether he is smart or dumb. But he has sat here and listened. I am quick to speak and slow to listen and this has been a great encouragement to me to listen more.'*

Wow! I said nothing and God used that to encourage him.

Oh, and it reminded me of this verse,

'Even the fool is thought wise if he keeps his mouth shut.'

Proverbs 17:28 NIVUK

# 39

# April 2006 - The Cold Rushing Waters of the Tigris River

Tülin and I continued on our trip to various places in eastern Turkey. On this day we were in Diyarbakır - the third largest city in the east. The city traces its origins back to the Stone Age. If you enjoy reading history, its ancient name was Amida.

At the end of the day, as I gazed into a mirror, white eyes stared back at me from a red face – it was a quiet testament that I had been wearing sunglasses all day. Although red, my face did not feel burnt, but my white eye sockets looked like something out of a sci-fi adventure. Tülin was likewise endowed with this new reddish-pink colouring, but without the white eyes.

It is not easy to get to this state of affairs. Indeed, it takes hours of diligent effort. For us the day began early, with the plan being to leave the house at 8:30 in the morning. Somewhere near that time, we descended the five floors from the flat where we were staying. There, waiting below, was a Volkswagen Transporter – a vehicle equipped with 12 or 13 seats.

The challenge was immediately apparent – there were over 13 people waiting to board the van. There were nigh on to twice that number clustered around the vehicle. They were a mixed bag of young people, older folks, and children — a swarm of children. And we had to take all the things needed for the outing. There were Bibles , song books, *mangal*[1], charcoal, meat, guitar, *saz*[2], the list went on.

As we waited by the van, more people drifted in. Then some people who had come and gone returned. Their hands were full of enough bread to feed a small army. Oh, and this mountain of bread would also have to find a place in the van.

You know, when you sit on a bench seat, if one leans forward and the next leans back, you can get more people on the seat than if you all sat back. And you can put children on your lap. People can sit in the passageway and if there is any open spot, someone can perch there. Hence, you can get near on 20 people in a 13 person van.

However, we could not take everyone who desired to board the van. The remaining people were to walk towards our destination, with another vehicle tasked to return and pick them up.

And so we were off. Tülin was squeezed in somewhere in the back with some ladies. I was blessed with a perch up front, sharing a seat with a gentleman. None of us knew how to get to where we were going. We knew the goal but not how to get there - nor exactly where it was. But we were off to link up with another vehicle whose driver show us the way. Or so we believed.

And so, having been loaded to capacity (a newly discovered capacity), we wound our way through the streets of Diyarbakır. From there, onto a divided road heading out of town towards the east. The road dropped into the Tigris River valley. We joined up with the car in the 'know' and followed them down into the bottom of the valley, across the Tigris and onwards.

Then there was a break in the divided roadway and the car made a U-turn. He was now headed back whence we came.

Hmmm.

We, like lambs to the slaughter, followed his manoeuvre. Now, we too, were returning along the same road. Soon we approached the bridge over the Tigris river again. Ah, the joy of being in the front seat. Unlike Tülin, lost in the jumble of humanity in the back, I could see where we were going. Well, in this case, where we had come from.

Just before the bridge, the car veered off the road onto a secondary gravel road. Or at least it had pretensions to being a secondary gravel road. We pulled alongside our guide car. We were told to go exactly five kilometres and then to turn off to the left down a simple farm track.

We were then abandoned by the car 'in the know' as they set off on other business. We, as instructed, continued our journey on this *almost* secondary gravel road. This road had seen the worst of the winter and the spring repairs, although possibly begun, were not yet completed. We bumped along, slowing over the bigger lumps, weaving around extended ruts, and making our way down the five kilometre stretch.

We came to a little village. Little it might be, but it had a mosque. The speakers on the minaret were sputtering sporadic bursts of noise. We stopped. We had an empty container. Now was the time to fill it full of water. So, off went the driver and another person to the mosque to fill the container up. While we waited, the minaret continued its barrage of indistinguishable noises. In the interlude, whilst waiting for the water party to return, slowly people emerged from the knot of passengers in the van. Some seeking relief, or maybe just air. When the water party returned, everyone piled back in and we continued our quest for the end of the five kilometre stretch.

As we approached the five kilometre point, we descended a gentle grade towards an even smaller collection of buildings. I refrain from calling this a village. The grade had seen the worst of the winter and was reduced to a tortured single track. At the bottom, before the road turned up through the collection of buildings, we had to slow. There were some serious disturbances in the road's surface to negotiate. Finally, we moved up the grade and made the five kilometre mark. There, to our left, was a simple field track.

A field trackway is the most basic of roads. That is, if you can apply the word 'road' even in the broadest sense of the word to this kind of *way*. The one encouraging thing for me was the evidence that a car had recently passed down the trackway. This gave me hope a car could successfully complete the course - *it did not occur to me it may not have been able to return*. And it gave hope that it was the correct track to our destination.

We headed off down the track but not at a great speed. The surface of this field track was, mostly not muddy, which was good. But there were parts where it was muddy and muddy equals slippery. And muddy means control is not automatically given, rather, you fight for it. There were a few muddy places.

Of course, a track is nothing if you don't have a gully running alongside of it. You know, a gully with dirt sides that could crumble or give way with the slightest provocation. It wasn't deep at two metres, and I didn't want an intimate introduction to it.

The track wasn't long by kilometre standards. But I didn't know where we were going and the gully was our constant companion… the upshot… it was long enough.

When we arrived at the end of the track, we could turn either left or right along the flood plain of the Tigris. We turned left, went a bit, and stopped. It felt like we stopped because we had lost the will to go on. It didn't *feel* like 'we have arrived'.

The restricted and compressed inhabitants of the van piled out — oh, and piled out and piled out. Cramped limbs were exercised. We stood in a clump around the van, not sure what the next step was or where to go.

Finally, a couple of young people emerged from the brush and showed the way. Everyone took something from the van. The meat, salad-makings, guitar, *saz, mangal*, water, bread were collected, and we headed off into the brush. Again, we were not really sure where we were heading or even if there was a path, but by faith we plodded on.

The flood plain was covered with sturdy shrubs and trees that could withstand the power of the river in flood. Being the first week of April, the trees were just budding, but they provided a canopy of welcome shade. The flood plain was not flat, however. It was broken up by piles of mostly grassed-over gravel. These piles ranged from a metre to three metres in height. Sometimes the piles were singles and sometimes they were lumped together, forming mini-ridges.

It was up and over one of these lumps that the stream of people from the van were, well, streaming. It was not always easy, whilst carrying a burden to negotiate even a single modest gravel hill. But, young and old alike, we successfully completed the trek. On the other side of the ridge, an appropriate spot had been chosen under a large budding tree.

The ground was thickly covered in grass, which was beautiful to look at but somewhat damp to sit upon. Blankets and carpets had been brought for this very reason. They were soon spread out on the ground, providing a spacious and dry place for all and sundry to rest.

Once we had all arrived, the place was put in order. But I could not see the river, so I headed off in a direction I thought would take me to the banks of the Tigris. As I neared the edge, I found there were no more trees, just shrubs; sturdy, wiry shrubs. But they were of sufficient height that I could still not see the river.

Finally, I made my way to the edge and there was the mighty Tigris. It was vigorously flowing from the right down to the left. At that point it was something like 40 metres in width. The water was rolling and flowing, revealing the speed and strength of the river. And, being April, the water was laden with the detritus of winter. It whisked past my vantage point on its long journey to the sea.

*The Dicle - in Turkish, the ancient Tigris river*

I paused and thought: it was within these frigid, swirling waters that a young man from the fellowship would soon be baptised.

I made my way back to the group. In keeping with eastern culture, we removed our shoes and took our places on the blankets and carpets. There were about 50 people assembled. A church elder began with a passage from the Psalms. Then we began singing various Turkish hymns to the Lord. We were accompanied by a guitar, a *saz*, and a *darbuka*[3]. We all know a guitar - it has become ubiquitous and international. But the other two instruments were Turkish. The *saz* is a kind of long-necked lute. The bowl of the *saz* is made from mulberry, juniper, beech, spruce or walnut. It has seven strings and is both plucked and strummed. This is both a 'classical' instrument and a 'folk' instrument.

The *darbuka* is a small hand drum, similar to a bongo drum. It has a distinctive sound and Turkish way of playing. It can make a variety of sounds and augment and complement many kinds of music. It, too, is ubiquitous in Turkey.

Being in the open air, I expected the sound to evaporate when we sang, but the combined voices merged, filling the space. It was as if the acoustics of the place amplified and resonated the sounds into a full-bodied, rich offering to the Lord. I found it both refreshing and encouraging.

At times the songs included two parts, with the ladies singing an echo. The sound was so rich. It was like twice the number of people singing.

After singing interspersed with prayer and verses, the speaker rose. Speaking from Matthew 13, he dwelt on the parables, focusing on the 'seed'. It encompassed both teaching and a challenge for the saints.

Then we all trooped to the edge of the Tigris. There the young man gave his testimony whilst standing in the swirling waters. Then two elders of the assembly entered the waters, awkwardly tottering as the bottom was rocky. The water was icy and the current was pulling at them as they moved into deeper water. Once at a suitable depth, the chap being baptised was asked the baptismal questions. With straightforward answers, he declared his identification with the death of Christ and the Resurrection.

The elders then guided his body below the surface of the waters. The cloudy waters of the Tigris swirled over him, tugging his body downstream. He rose out of the water, a testimony of the power of God to save fallen man. The saints gathered at the shore, rejoiced with him, and burst into song.

Following this, we returned for a celebration picnic. Several *mangals* were set up, and the work of the day began. The meat was forced on the skewers and two men parked themselves behind the *mangals*. They began cooking up a mountain of meat. The ladies took an enormous pile of vegetables and combined them into a pinnacle of salad.

The moment arrived when everything was ready. The salad was piled on a large tray, and the meat, covered in bread, was heaped onto two large metal trays. One meat tray was brought and placed at my feet – the other at the feet of the speaker. We laughed and joked, declaring, well, two people had their food.

After a prayer of thanksgiving, a swarm of children descended on the waiting food. They, impatiently, were thrusting their empty plates forward. There were little people everywhere, plates at the ends of eager arms. The servers grabbed a handful of meat, a handful of salad and dumped them on the plates. The children were concerned solely with filling their plates and, oh, getting some bread. ***No meal in Turkey is complete until there is bread.*** The children were less concerned with where they were standing or where their feet were going. I could foresee, thankfully only in my mind's eye, some child stepping in the second tray of meat. It didn't happen, but almost, almost…

Finally, all the children had full plates and it was the turn of the adults. A steady flow of adults flocked up with empty plates. They retreated with plates laden with barbecued chicken, salad, and a piece of bread torn from the long flat bread brought from the city.

There was still meat, salad and bread. Unfortunately for us, it seemed we had run out of plates.

Now as a diabetic I had been pushing the envelope of what I can endure and how long I can go without some sustenance. I never want to inconvenience people or make a fuss. But it had been a long time since breakfast – a very long time. I wasn't doing terribly well and there were no more plates.

It wasn't just Tülin and I - the speaker had been distracted with talking with various individuals and he, too, was left plate-less. This was noticed and there was suddenly a flurry of activity. More plates were found, promptly laden with a generous portion of meat, salad and bread.

The meat was not only full of flavour, but it was like a glass of cold water on a hot summer's day. It made an immediate impact on my low blood sugar.

After our meal in the shade of the budding tree, the young people went off to play a game of dodge ball. Others went to play with Frisbees and still others went for gentle walks among the trees and shrubs.

Tülin had spent most of the day sitting on one of the three chairs – her hip not giving permission to sit on the carpets or blankets on the ground. I went off on a quiet walk by the waters of the Tigris river.

After this time of gentle activity, we began to gather. The little groupings of twos and threes that have been chatting together slowly formed a large group.

As a group, we chatted a bit. Then an Armenian girl whose family had migrated to Canada – and she had later returned to Turkey – sang a song in Armenian. Then a chap sang a song in Zaza[4]. They were accompanied by the *saz* and *darbuka*.

Then the hymn books were called for and we began singing hymns. But as we were only using the *saz*, hymns most appropriate to the *saz* were being selected.

Unfortunately, I didn't receive a hymn book. So, I was limited to being more a listener than a singer.

As more people joined in, more books were distributed and I was a recipient of one of these. Instant promotion from listener to participant. The songs were being suggested at a furious rate. People were suggesting the next song to sing after the one after the one we are about to sing. Great!

As the day was drawing to a close, we sang the last song. Then came a general clean up of the area – all our trash was going back with us. When all was ready, we, each carrying something, trooped back to the vehicles. But this time we knew the way. And with all our coming and going, now there was a path. Vehicles were repacked.

Tülin was squeezed in the same vehicle we came in, but I was given a bit of a space on another vehicle for the return journey.

I can't say much about our return journey, for I was consigned to the back of a van on the return leg. But I know it involved the track with its muddy points of interest and the road that aspired to be a secondary gravel road.

Hence, red face and white eyes for me, and pink/red face and arms for Tülin.

But more lasting and more important, there were two visitors that day. One who had travelled five hours from Gaziantep to join in. He had read the New Testament and seemed to have a good grasp of the essentials. He warmly took part in the various activities, singing the hymns, and listening intently to the sharing. At the end of the day he said if he had known what it was going to be like, he would have brought his wife. He was positively impressed with this day in the life of the Church.

The other chap had travelled a shorter distance, hadn't read any of the New Testament, and was looking, most likely, for work. Nevertheless, regardless of what brought him into our midst, he too had a double dose. He saw, up close and personal, a full day with Christians who love one another and love the Lord.

# 40

# April 2006 - Off to an Ancient Monastery

Tülin, I, our travelling companion, and the leader of the church in Diyarbakır, climbed into the van and headed further south and east. We were going off the beaten track and would visit places seldom seen.

As we headed south from Diyarbakır, rolling plains spread out on all sides. The Tigris river valley was slipping from sight as we went. Soon the surrounding landscape was dyed with deep shades of green. This was mute testimony to the rich fertility of this area. I knew where we were going, (that is, the destination) but I did not know the route we would be taking. It was exciting to be travelling across Mesopotamia, the ancient fertile crescent; the land between the Tigris and Euphrates rivers.

Traffic was light and we were making good time. But when you do not know the distances, you don't know if you are an hour from your destination or three. In fact, it proved to be closer to three.

*The fields south of Diyarbakır*

After a while, the fertile plain gave way to stony hills. When I say 'stony', what I really mean is 'more stones than anything else'. There seemed to be little soil and the bedrock was exposed on all sides. The hills grew in height as we wound our way through narrowing valleys and up and over ridges. This was the antithesis of the previous vista. There everything was dressed in green and with the promise of crops to come. This, however, was dressed in stony grey and devoid of promise. Well, as much as I could see.

Sitting as I was at the very back, my view was limited. I was behind the driver and his passenger in the front seats, and also behind Tülin and a young lady in the middle seat. Hence, my view was limited to what flashed past the side windows. There was not much warning of what was coming, and if it was something near, it would be visible for the briefest of moments. I gathered we would pass by Mardin on our way to the ancient city of *Midyat*[1] and from thence on to our accommodation for the night.

We skirted the ancient city of Mardin. It is perched on a steep hill, looking down on the endless plains of Mesopotamia. The old city is made of stone on terraces, and is a fascinating place to visit. However, we approached from the back side, the opposite side of the old city. Hence, we could not see it, nor could we see how the hill sharply drops off to the vast plain and that the plain then disappears over the horizon. Our brief encounter with Mardin was in such a manner that there was little to see.

After passing the back of Mardin, we were off, heading east, down another valley. The road then climbed a steep grade and emerged out of the valley. We were in a region of gently rolling rocky hills. These hills were interspersed with small green valleys. Every shred of fertile land was given over to agriculture.

I have found when travelling down a new road, even a short distance can seem to take a long time. So, in this way, it was difficult to appreciate the length of the journey. But in the fullness of time we reached the city of Midyat.

Midyat is a town that has a special place in my heart and mind. Years earlier, Tülin and I watched a filmstrip[2] that featured an event that happened in Midyat. I'm afraid young people will need to search for 'filmstrip' as it is now an ancient term. With a filmstrip, you would project pictures on to a screen or wall together with a cassette tape providing the commentary. My, how things have changed.

The filmstrip contained a section on Midyat and the events that took place in this town many years ago. At the turn of the 20th century, there was a civil war and fighting in the east of the failing Ottoman Empire. In those days, the Christians of Midyat were gathered together. The men were separated from the women and children, and taken down to the well. There they were killed and their bodies dumped into the well. As they were led to the execution place, the women and children followed them out. And, in this most painful time, the ladies made an ululation[3] - a sound of praise as their men were going to meet God.

OM (Operation Mobilisation) organised young people from around the world to give their summer holidays to travel to other countries and share the Good News of Jesus. OM made this filmstrip to share the need in Turkey.

Now in Midyat, the thing that struck me was the number of work-shops preparing white stone blocks. I love stone buildings and I had arrived at a centre of stone buildings and stone work.

The local stone, when first quarried, is off-white and when freshly cut is fairly soft and hence workable. However, once exposed to the air, it hardens and over time changes from a soft to a hard stone.

We parked up to get some things to take to our destination. In the city centre the State was building a new mosque out of richly worked local stone. There was a memorial, again built of the local stone and heavily worked. Everywhere we looked we saw the generous usage of this stone. I came across the local tourism office, and, yes, it too was built of the local stone. It was all impressive.

When I returned to the car, Tülin and the young lady commented that there was not a single woman on the streets. There were none. No women. Not by themselves, not accompanied by a male family member or husband. There were not even the heavily veiled ladies in the full black tent-like covering. A quick glance at my watch told me it was 6:30 in the evening and this wasn't time for ladies to be out and about in Midyat. We didn't know that, so it was good Tülin had opted to stay in the van when I went to do some business.

After the rest of the party returned, we resumed our quest. It was past dusk now, so we would arrive in the dark. We departed Midyat heading in a south-easterly direction.

Another half hour down the two-lane road and we reached the turnoff. Our driver swung the van across the road and we began going up the hill on the side of the low valley. The road was narrower than the one we had been using, but if there was oncoming traffic we could have passed without difficulty.

In any event, on this road there was no oncoming traffic. There was, in fact, no other traffic at all. The distance was about five kilometres... At about four kilometres we could see the shape of our destination. There, in the murk, a large black lump on top of a hill was still discernible.

Finally, we pulled up to a four metre high stone wall that encircled the complex. To the left was a wide, massive gate built in the classical style with a rounded arch. It was decorated with white stone and a massive, securely fastened, solid steel door. We stopped in front of another, smaller, gate. It, too, was set in a finely stone carved arch. And it too was also tightly secured for the night. The gate was made of wrought iron, with decorative leaves interwoven with the bars. This was both extremely pleasing to look at and a secure barrier to our forward progress.

The sign beside the sealed gate declared the visiting hours. We were well outside of them. The chap who had arranged the visit leaped out of the vehicle and went in search of a bell. I don't know if he found a bell or not, but he came back looking for his phone.

A quick call and someone was dispatched to open the gate. Well, our visit was prearranged, so even at this late hour, and in the dark, someone was coming down to open the gate.

We waited.

Our gate-opener was coming, but slowly as it was a long way from the main building.

Finally, someone could be seen walking down the drive. He opened the large gate and we breezed through. We drove up the drive and across a massive parking lot to another gate in the wall of the complex.

Like the outer wall, this gate was set in a massive stone wall towering some four plus metres above us. The chap who had opened the outer gate had left this door open for us. We grabbed our luggage and began, well lugging our burdens.

We traipsed through the gate, across a stone clad courtyard, and up a double set of stairs. Then across another expanse of stone cladding and up another set of stairs. This led us across a shorter stone clad surface with a left turn and up yet more stairs. Now, we traipsed across a stone clad terrace and we arrived at the door to the Metropolitan's[4] reception room.

Example of the stone work at Mor Gabriel[5]

Welcome to Mor Gabriel. This is a Süriyani[6] (Syrian Orthodox) Monastery founded in 397. Yes, that is the correct date - nothing is missing. That is 1,609 years ago. This is one old, ancient place.

I did not know what the accommodation would be like in such an ancient monastery. I guess I was expecting a small, rather primitive monk's cell, with a hard bed and it being cold and damp. I was surprised that my wife and our other female travelling companion were allowed into the monastery at all.

In the end, we were shown to some very nice, very modern, en suite rooms.

In the morning light, we looked out from the fortress-like complex on the vista surrounding us. Here believers had settled, studied, prayed, lived, and died for hundreds and hundreds and hundreds of years.

Once this complex was in the border region between the Roman and the Persian empires. Armies from one side or the other would ravage the land, taking what they wanted. And, invariably, after taking what they wanted, they destroyed what was left. It is no wonder the buildings are built with massive defensive structures. Even today there is hostility and resentment towards Christians and the defensive nature of the building is still required.

Despite the hostility and pressure on all sides, high above the central church in the complex, adorning the bell tower is a large orthodox cross. It has been constructed in such a way that it is clearly a cross. Regardless of your angle, you can clearly see the cross and at night this is lit, shining as a beacon in the night.

So, it is for us. We, by our life style and values, are to shine as a beacon set on a hill. Now observers can like or even hate us and people may threaten us from time to time. Indeed, there are examples where individuals have enacted their threats, but we are to shine like a beacon in the night. Here on a hill in the Tur Abdin area,[7] the cross of Christ shines forth in the darkness from the highest point of the monastery - it shines as an enduring message of hope, life and freedom. And so, we, as individuals, too, need to shine in this world of ours, offering hope, life and freedom.

# 41

# April 2006 - Uncle Yohanna

As we departed through the gate of the Mor Gabriel Monastery[1], the vista from the hilltop spread out before us. In the highlands, the ancient region known as Tur Abdin lay before us. And there standing by the side of the road, were two ancients. I did not know how old they were by the calendar, but by the look of them, well, Abraham and Sarah came to mind. They were hitchhiking and our driver stopped to welcome them on board.

'Where are you going?' he asked.

'Midyat' came the gravelly response from the greybeard.

'We are going in the other direction - we can take you to the main road, then we will turn and go to Midin.'

'I will go to Midin too,' exclaimed the other ancient.

After the five kilometre descent, we arrived at the main road. The female ancient descended from the van to await a passing bus which would come and take her the rest of the way to Midyat. She looked completely at sea with these arrangements but climbed out of the van and went to the side of the road.

We turned left and, leaving a somewhat bewildered looking ancient by the side of the road, continued on our journey to Midin. Immediately, one of our travelling companions began sharing the Good News with the one remaining ancient. I don't know how much he understood. But for the duration of the trip, the Good News was explained to him. This was probably the first time in his long, and looking at him, hard life, that he had heard this.

After some forty minutes, we swung off the main road and down towards the village of Midin. It was a simple collection of stone-built houses, outbuildings, barns, and sheds. They all clustered around a slight rise in the ground. Standing proud in the centre of the buildings, was a Syrian Orthodox church. This is the last 'all Syrian Orthodox' village in Turkey.

Having arrived in the village of Midin, our ancient passenger disembarked. He was continuing on to the Muslim village down the road.

We continued on the road that circled the village. We had almost gone around the entire village to arrive at our destination - the home of Yohanna Amca[2] (Uncle Yohanna) and his family.

*Midin in the south east of Turkey*

Yohanna Amca is in his seventies and is a Süryani protestant believer. He lives in a vast sea of Islam and on a small island of Süryani Orthodox. Through good time and bad, he has maintained his testimony and freely shared the Good News to all and sundry. He has a reputation for honesty and straight dealings in the village.

But, situated as they are deep in the South East, there is not much opportunity for fellowship outside the family. Yohanna Amca is the family patriarch. He lives with his son, wife, and their small tribe of children. Hence, it is a special blessing when believers make the journey to their little village. In the evening, our plan was to gather to speak of the Lord, read scripture, sing spiritual songs, and our travelling companion would speak from the Word.

As we had arrived, we piled out of the van and entered through the strong, double steel doors that open to a central courtyard. We entered and the overpowering smell of animals overwhelmed me. The animals and their associated smells enveloped me like a smothering blanket. It was here, in the courtyard, that the goats were stabled at night. Oh, and the chickens were housed at courtyard level in the rooms on the right. There were rooms also on the left - but I did not investigate their function.

We proceeded across the courtyard, it's pungent scent filling our nostrils. We greeted Yohanna Amca with a warm embrace and, as Scripture says, a holy kiss. We proceeded up the narrow concrete stairs to the first floor. The rooms on the first floor, on the left as you enter the courtyard, were the family rooms. On the right was the family sitting room, kitchen, formal sitting room and formal dining room.

We slipped our shoes off at the door and proceeded to the formal sitting room. Once again, we greeted each other. We sat down and talk quickly passed from the 'How are you?' to spiritual topics.

As it was mid-afternoon, it was suggested we take a walk, and so the men of our party set out. The 'strolling' group consisted of we, the visitors, the son of Yohanna Amca, and a young man who had returned from Europe. This young man had decided to once again live in the village.

On one side of the village, a gorge began, and over a short distance it deepened and widened. It quickly became not only an impassible barrier from one side to the other but an impressive sight. It was into this gorge we entered for our stroll.

First, we examined a rock spring with crystal clear water. This was once the source of water for the village before the State installed running water. In days gone by, the ladies of the village would descend into the gorge to collect their daily water. They would enter the spring cave, load up with water for the family, and then carry it back to their homes.

From the spring we continued travelling down the gorge to rock carved openings. Hm, there was a difference of opinion here. Some said 'homes' and one said 'graves'. Whatever the truth, there was a cluster of rooms hewn out of the living rock on the sides of the gorge. They were of different sizes, but a common plan was an entrance with an open common space in the centre. Then there were between one and three bed-like platforms carved out of the remaining walls. These bed-like platforms were sometimes 'singles' and sometimes 'doubles'. This supported the rock home interpretation, as you would not normally bury people side by side. Well, at least that was the way it struck me.

Most 'of these spaces' were single rooms with platforms. There was one that seemed to have several rooms. However, the skeleton of a horse lying in one of the rooms put me off from a more extensive investigation.

The sun was gently shining and it was warm enough to take my jacket off. The grass, that tender green of spring, and the gentle buzz of insects made this a perfect spring day.

We climbed up out of the gorge and made our way back towards the village. There were some almond trees in a small grove. We picked the tender young almonds. They were a bitter-sweet treat, plucked fresh from the tree.

On our return to the courtyard home, we were ushered into the formal dining room. The 'we' being ushered in comprised us, the guests, plus Yohanna Amca and his son. His wife and children ate elsewhere. Well, even with this reduced number, we filled all the spaces. The dining room table was made of concrete legs and substructure, with a large single slab of marble laid on top. There was no way to extend this table.

Yohanna Amca and his son provided the food service. First there was fresh bread baked that afternoon in the outdoor oven. This oven was preheated with a wood fire inside. Once the oven was at the right temperature, the lady of the home would take the dough and stick it inside the oven on the sides. It would bake in there. When it was ready, she would remove it. She would do several days' supply at one go, as it is an unbearably hot task. I mean, the oven is hot enough to bake bread. She has to put her arm and hands into it to put the dough on the walls and to remove the bread.

So, we were treated to fresh bread, a large pan of cooked meat, two kinds of pilaf - one bulgar and one rice - and vegetables. A veritable feast.

When we had eaten our fill, we retired to the formal sitting room for the chief business of the visit. Because visitors from outside the village were rare and it is even rarer for foreigners to come, some of Yuhanna Amca's friends from the village came as well. The lady of the house and the older children also joined with us. We read from the Word and shared. We prayed and then broke bread together, ending with a hymn.

By the time the spiritual feast was over, it was gone midnight.

Sleeping accommodation was the same room we were meeting in. Three settees folded down to make beds. This accommodated three of our number. Two foam mattresses were put on the floor for the remaining two. Some changed into pj's. Others slept in the clothes they stood up in. We all crawled under the blankets and passed into the land of Nod.

The following morning, we partook of a rich 'Turkish breakfast'. We had more village bread, homemade goat's cheese, olives, jam and tea. After our repast, we said our goodbyes. For us, it was one more stop among many. For them, it was the last of Christian fellowship until someone else makes the trip. The nearest believers were four hours away by car.

*Yohanna Uncle - front and centre*

Again, taking our places in the van, we headed out of the village and back onto the road. Travel that day would be intense. We would travel first to Mardin. We were visiting not the town, which was on our way, but another monastery[3]. After visiting the folks there, we were to return to Diyarbakir. Oh, yes, and to arrive in time for our travelling companions to make their afternoon flight back to their city.

# 42

# May 2006 - Slip, Slide, and Away... Almost

Normally, it had taken us about half an hour to travel from Izmir (Smyrna[1]) to Selçuk (Ephesus[2]). But today we had a different starting point. It was going to take us an hour as we laboriously wound our ways through the warrens and alleyways of Izmir. We would be late for the Sunday meeting. But I've learned over the years that if you are going to be late, *you are going to be late*. There is no value in being stressed, rushing, or trying to make up for lost time. If I exceed the posted speed limit, the resulting speeding ticket rarely provides a wonderful opportunity to share the Good News. My error was in the time we departed. Hence, I have learned to learn from mistakes like this for future reference and to drive sensibly.

The motorway between the two cities is marvellous. As it leaves Izmir behind, you enter a large plain between the mountains. It is probably 50 kilometres long and ranging from 1 to 20 kilometres wide. It is narrow at both ends and wide in the middle. The road is well engineered and so straight as to be monotonous. It travels straight down the plain and then swings up onto the low shoulder of the mountains on the right. Traffic was light on this Sunday morning and we were making as good speed as you would expect.

Being spring, there were roving rain showers lurking in the mountains. Occasionally, they would make a foray across the plain, their long skirts of rain draping down from the cloud head, obscuring the fields below in their localised tempest.

We encountered a bit of rain during the journey, but nothing of consequence. We arrived at the point where we must part company with the motorway. We paid our toll and then started to change to a good four-lane road to take us to Selçuk. Here the valley has constricted to its narrowest point. The motorway exit is under the shadow of 'Keçi[3] Kale' or 'Goat Castle'. The castle is perched on a pinnacle of the mountain on the west side. From this majestic view point in the past it controlled the trade routes below.

We left the toll booth and the road was wet with rain. Here was clear physical evidence of a recent visit by one of the rain squalls. The sun had not abandoned us and was shining on us as it peeked out from between the clouds. The road curved off to the left. From there it split, with one lane dropping off to the right to go up the plain towards Torbalı and the other lane continuing on the left-hand curve to join the dual carriageway that would take us to Selçuk.

But before us, there was a car – caught on the horns of a dilemma. It seemed to me they were questioning: do they go right or do they go left? To make matters worse, they had stopped to ponder the point. However, for me, there was nothing to ponder. I knew where we were going and it was off to the left.

But as we approached their nearly stationary car, they decided that left was better than right and slowly got under way.

The speed sign was clear, 70 kph. But immediately following it was another stating: 60 kph. But I had sped up to swing past the chap as he was just starting up. I was not so much slowing to 60 as still speeding up to pass.

We swung by them and crossed the bridge over the motorway we had just left. I was powering into a left-hand curve.

Now I don't know what caused the events that followed. Tülin was of the opinion that I touched the brakes. I could have touched the brakes. I do not remember doing so. But it is true, I was going faster than the posted limit. That I know.

Everything looked and felt good. I felt no premonition of things about to deviate from the known to the unknown, from the controlled to the uncontrolled. I had no inkling that things were about to move from the pleasant to the unpleasant. I like comfortable but we were headed to the decidedly uncomfortable.

As we entered the curve, all was fine.

Then the back end of the car rebelled. It was like it felt it was too tedious to always be trailing after the front end. It seems the back end of the car thought the time appropriate to swing out and try to pass the front of the car. It was going to pass on the right-hand side.

I confess, this was not expected. I must add, it was also not welcomed. It was very unwelcome indeed. The slip road was not wide — a single lane with paved shoulders.

And there was a definite curve going off to the left. Where it was going was obscured by the bend in the road. Truth be told, *I, as the driver, was going too fast*. But there was nothing to be done about that now. As is so often in cases like this, the answer was, *'not to be going too fast.'* **But we were going too fast**.

Years of driving in snowy conditions brought back some instinctive responses. I turned the steering wheel in the direction of the skid. This was right. But I turned a bit too quickly, and a bit too energetically. The concept was good and the action appropriate, but the execution was clumsy and overdone.

The back end of the car was enjoying its newfound freedom.

Although ham-handed, my abrupt handling of the steering wheel brought the back end of the car back to where it belonged. But not to be deterred, the back end kept on going.

It was like it reasoned: if it could not pass on the right, then it would have a go at passing on the left. A new sideways skid developed to the left-hand side this time.

Now this was not the turn of events that I had hoped for. The road was narrow and bordered on both sides by hefty steel guard rails. I could see where the rails on the left had been put to the test. They were bowed outwards, where something big and heavy and moving at speed had interacted with them. You know, something like a… car, maybe. This was not an encouraging sign.

Those who know me well know that when things go from bad to worse, I laugh. Hey, if the choice is to laugh or cry, you may as well laugh. At this point in time, however, *I was silent*. My attention was elsewhere. Neither a laugh nor chuckle escaped from my lips.

I'm not sure what Tülin was doing, as she also was silent.

The car, still moving at some speed, was descending upon the warped guard rail. And, against what I wanted to do, I turned the steering wheel into the slide. That is, towards the guard rail. It was close and coming closer every second.

Yikes!

My mind recalled that the shortest distance between two points is a straight line and I had just aimed at the guard rail.

And so we were sliding, far too fast, towards the guard rail. All I knew to do and all my experience told me what to do, I had done. I had turned the tyres towards the skid and then all I could do was wait.

In response to the correction I made, the back end of the car, grumpily, snapped back again. It quickly traversed from the left, all the way to the right. However, I had again over-corrected. I was motivated by the sight of the bent and twisted steel of the guard rail.

My over-zealous application gave impetus to the back end of the car. It was not just back to where it belonged but again skidding to the right side.

Well, the back end was having an exciting flight between either extreme. I hoped it was happy.

Now this wasn't good, but it was better. There was more distance to slide as we headed for the right-hand guard rail. We were nearly on the left-hand rail when it snapped over.

I turned the wheel back towards the skid. My mind now filling with the admonition – not too much this time, little by little.

So I inched the wheel around in the direction of the skid. Slowly, slowly, and the back end of the car capitulated. It once again took up station at the back of the car. Thankfully, its frenetic bid for free-dom, for free expression, for dominance in giving direction to the car, was over. It now quietly submitted to the old order and meekly followed along.

Now, as we were travelling down the middle of the lane, the bulk of the curve behind us, we carried on in silence. Mind you, by this time we were travelling at a slower speed. For the first time since the fun began, my foot moved off the floor and onto the petrol pedal. It was time to carry on to our destination.

It was... ah... exciting. And no, I don't really want to do it again. Actually, I didn't want to do it the first time.

It would seem this minor event is an example of what I am feeling at the moment. I know where we are going. But I can't always see around the curve. Sometimes things go out of 'my' control. But they are never out of 'His' control.

For quite some time I have been asking, *'How I might be most effective?'* in the Lord. How can I, who I am and the gifts and abilities I have, be effective? Of all the Christian workers in the country, a dispro-portionate number are in the big cities. Istanbul has the lion's share.

So, the question I asked myself and I asked the Lord was, 'Is there another location where we can better serve the Lord? Is there a place where I can pursue what I believe to be the calling the Lord has laid on us? And what is that calling? - that we may be an encouragement, a help, a blessing, to the work of the Lord in a Turkish fellowship?'

As is often the case in life, we know where we are going – ultimately. But there is a curve. We can't see around the corner. All the while we want to proceed. But I need to keep the speed in check and see what the Lord has for us.

# 43

# June 2006 - Which Side is Right

Tülin and I had returned to the United Kingdom for a special engagement. Our time was to be brief.

Travelling as we do between countries, we must deal with the reality that in some places you drive on the right and in others you drive on the left. With time and experience, I have devised a foolproof method to keep me on the correct side of the road.

It works simply, regardless of what country I am in. The rule: the driver's side of the car is always nearest the centre of the road. Of course, this depends on the car being appropriate to the country. With this method, it does not matter how wide or narrow the road is. As the driver, my side of the car must always be nearest the centre.

Even on a narrow road, where the car takes up most of the road surface, this works. You meet an oncoming vehicle, you will put the driver's side of the car nearest the centre of the road. I should see asphalt, not bushes.

It works a treat.

Well, it did until… until the day I took my son's bicycle out for a spin. There I was, going down a narrow-ish road. There were cars parked on either side and facing both directions. Then there came two oncoming cars.

Which way do I go - which way *do I go*?

In a car the steering wheel would be *the clue*. There are two sides: one with a steering wheel and one without. My rule says keep the driver near the centre of the road. But on a bicycle there are no sides. I am in the centre of the conveyance. Ahhhh…

This dilemma overwhelmed my mind with one thought: 'What was I to do?' There I am in the middle of the road and traffic is coming towards me. They, too, are basically travelling down the middle of the road. The road is narrow. I must turn some direction. *But do I go left or do I go right?*

In the end, I decided that any way is better than proceeding in indecision. I veered violently to the right, which was the wrong side. But I was out of the way, which at that moment was the most important point.

So, I have the simple answer for cars, vans or any motorised four wheeled conveyance. But for bicycles, I simply have to learn. Depending on the country, I have to know ahead of time which side is correct. When here - go there, and when somewhere else, go there.

It is not nearly as elegant. And it is not so foolproof. But better to have a plan than to figure it out at the time.

# 44

# July 2006 - 'Yr Wyddgrug´ - Say What??

'Yr Wyddgrug'. The sign flashed by the window quickly. But my mind reeled in the attempt to find sounds to go with what my eyes saw.

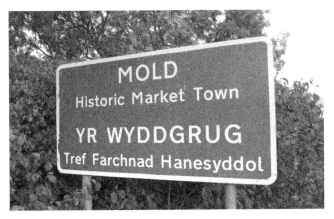

*This sign was a bit more explanatory than the first one we saw*

This sign seemed to be the opposite of Turkish. I do not know Welsh nor its alphabet. But I know Turkish is a phonetic language.

Each letter holds a single value ***in all instances***. The letters do not change. And every letter is pronounced.

Hence, if someone learns the sounds of the letters, they can 'pronounce' words in Turkish. They may not know Turkish, but a Turk who hears them will understand what they are saying.

Ah, but this was not Turkish. And for me it was a mind-befuddling collection of consonants occasionally interrupted by a stray vowel. My mind went blank, my tongue went limp. I hadn't the vaguest idea of what sounds I should produce based on the characters before my eyes.

Tülin, however, is much better at spelling and sounding out words than I am. I fall at the lowest of hurdles. She sails on, pronouncing words she has never seen with an ease and grace that is a beauty to behold. Whilst I fumble around squeaking and squawking, she lets the unfamiliar words roll off her tongue. Many times she has cleared up, for me, the mystery of how to say the new word. She is great.

But now even she had met her match.

It is not saying much when I say, 'I do not know how to say…' That is kind of my normal, default setting. But for Tülin to be stumped by a new constellation of, well, consonants, now that is saying something.

'Hebryngwr' another sign swung into view. My mouth puzzled over what it would do with an 'ngwr' – I still don't know. Tülin was likewise rendered speechless.

Excellent word – no doubt. Full of meaning – I'm sure. But not for us.

'Ffyrdd drwodd' – double ffs and double dds; I'm at sea here – lost…

'Dim marciau ffordd' – normally we encountered an over abundance of consonants, tightly grouped together. This left me vainly groping in the dark for the sounds to link those little guys together.

But now we had vowels, a whole torrent of them. It was like reciting vowels as a child - a - e - i - o - u, and sometimes y, for a child it was a meaningless jumble of letters, but used to teach the vowels. Here I was confronted with 'iau' – 'iau' what am I going to do with that?

I know... I will sit in silence — Tülin, too.

Now, let me be clear, there is nothing wrong with the signs. And I must emphasise that there is nothing wrong with the language. But we, lacking even the most rudimentary understanding of the Welsh language, were totally bereft of understanding what the signs meant. Indeed, they may have provided good directions and important warnings - just not to us. **We lacked the knowledge**. Nor did we possess the tools or the training necessary to benefit from the signs posted at the side of the road. A six-year-old Welsh child would do better than us.

All was not lost, as the signs were bi-lingual – unlike us.

Ultimately, the directions were understood, and the warnings heeded. But to appreciate the beauty of the Welsh language and the delightful sounds and nuance of the language, the translation into English doesn't help. The meaning is there, the beauty is lost. The understanding has come, but the allure and the grace of the language are veiled - hidden from our view.

Okay, we understood the translation, but we lost so much. Yes, we lost something in the renderings of simple road signs.

And so, here in this land of Turkey, our goal is not to present something veiled and hard to understand. Nor is our goal to present something translated from a foreign and confusing tongue. We aim to see native-born men and women expressing the Good News in the Turkish language. They will naturally use local idiom and speech as they declare the wonders and beauty of God. The message is of eternal importance, touching the mind, the heart and the soul of every believer. And for the Turks, that means, in Turkish...

If, in the Grace of the Lord, we have the opportunity to once again travel in the beautiful Welsh countryside, I would first like to learn at least some rudiments of the Welsh language. To taste some sweetness of the language, to dip even a wee bit into the well of that ancient tongue would be a delight.

# 45

# August 2006 - How Hot is Hot?

Tülin mused to herself, 'How much do you genuinely need to live? How many belongings do you *really* need?' as she began packing for our month in Antakya (that is, Antioch on the Orontes River in the Bible). She thought, 'Do I really need to pack eight shirts?'

We had decided, (well, conditionally decided, would be more accurate) to think and pray about moving to Antakya for well over a year. By the end of the year, we felt it was 'right in the Lord' to go.

I had been disappointed and frustrated in trying to make Turkish language videos for the Turkish church. I felt like I was spinning my tyres and making no headway. So, this would be a genuine change in focus and activity.

There was, however, a concern over how well we could adapt to a tropical climate. This is about as far south as you can go — and still be in Turkey.

Tülin paused and considered. 'That's what I normally pack. One set per day, times seven, for a week. There would be one to wear when the other 7 were being washed.' But it's HOT in Antakya. She knew from our experience living in Selçuk for a year that clothes dry quickly. So, now she was considering how many skirts she needed to pack. Surely three was enough; one to wear, one to wash and one for 'emergencies'.

She thought, 'Once we have arrive in Antakya, I wonder, do we really need more than two plates? We are two people. Isn't one pot and a frying pan enough?'

And so her thoughts were occupied with the many practical decisions to be made. Some things were essential and others were not. We were only going for a month - but she didn't want to forget something necessary.

Our journey began in Istanbul in the north-west of Turkey. Our destination was Antakya in the south-east. Although it was only about one thousand kilometres, it took us three days to complete the journey. We passed over mountain passes, through evergreen forests, across a high mountain plateau, and along the side of a vast salt lake. The last day included a trip up over the coastal Amanos Mountains from Iskenderun. Iskenderun was first called Alexandria when Alexander the Great founded it in 333 BC.

At the mountain pass, known in the Bible as the Syrian Gates, we gazed down from the dizzying heights. I carefully drove down the road as it snaked back and forth from the high pass into the distant valley floor below. In ancient times, part of the valley was a shallow lake where the Seleucid Kings kept their war elephants. But this shallow lake was a constant source of malaria - blighting the valley. Today it is has been drained and a fertile green plain stands where the lake once was.

Once we made our descent, we turned basically south towards Antakya, going down the valley to the modern/ancient city. The arrangements were for us to make our way directly to the church meeting place, which was to be our home for our visit to Antakya.

Thing is, I'd been to the meeting place twice in the last year and always as a passenger, never driving there. So, I decided to work from known landmarks. I headed off for the road that leads to the cave grotto called St Peters. That is where, *they say*, the first believers gathered. A friend raised questions about that claim. It is possible, said he, but in the very early days of the church there was no persecution in Antakya.

Whatever the truth may be, I headed for the road at the base of the mountain containing the cave. Thankfully, I could see the mountain and the base was clear. So, I reasoned, it was a landmark I could work from.

Once there, we headed deeper into the town on a narrow, busy road. This road is called in Turkish 'Salvation Street'. It runs parallel to the mountain. At a point where all seemed right to me, we turned right into a more dense part of the old city. Down this street, and by the Grace of God, we found the incredibly narrow street we needed. It led into the warren of medieval lanes that comprise the old quarter. The old quarter is full of stone houses with private courtyards. It also contained our destination – the church meeting place. As I turned up the constricted lane, I was glad we had both a small and an old car. We drove up about a hundred metres and parked outside the meeting place.

Now, as this is an old area of town, you basically have walls of either one or two stories high. There was a single solid steel door marking the entrance. We clambered out of the car. Although we were drenched in sweat from our travels, we eagerly stepped through the open steel door to the church.

Now when I say church please understand I am not referring to the genuine sense of the word. The Church comprises people, not bricks and stones. And, I know the true Church is not tied to any geographical point or structure. I know that Church is not a particular architectural design. It is good that I know this, as the building we entered did not look like a typical church.

But it was merely the meeting place - for when the church gathered.

When we passed through the steel door, we arrived at what was formerly an old stone 'house'. It was this rented stone-built courtyard house where the church now gathers.

Immediately, as you crossed the threshold of the steel door, you were in a dressed stone-flagged courtyard. To the left was the old stone wing with six tall windows crowned with simple stone arches. There were two wooden doors, one of which was used as a window and the other as a door. Formerly there were two rooms, hence two different doors. The rooms were combined to create a larger meeting room for the Church.

To my eyes, it looked wonderful - but then I love stone and stone-built structures.

On the right was the opposite wing, also built of stone. But, I hasten to add, not handsomely dressed stone as the meeting room. It was a simpler building. It was made with plain field stone walls, plastered over and painted off-white. This wing comprised two small rooms, a narrow kitchen and a loo/shower.

The first room was for our exclusive use while we stayed in Antakya. It was our bedroom and my workroom. I had brought a project with me to work on. The video work was continuing.

I planned to edit the film 'Joni' whilst here. The story of Joni follows a young girl's plight after she dived into some water and broke her neck. It follows her life as she came to grips with being a quadriplegic.

The second room was for the young people to use. The kitchen was a narrow corridor but with a sink, cooker and fridge. It was basic but sufficient. But remember, this was a man writing about the kitchen. The loo was also a long narrow corridor-like room. It had an *alafranga* toilet. Uh, as I said already, that would be an European/North American style toilet. There was also an electric shower with the shower head on the wall. Walls and floors were all tiled – it was a wet room. All rooms opened on to the courtyard. In order to get from room to room, you were required to take a side trip to the courtyard.

Mind you, it was a dressed stone-flagged courtyard, so it was a pleasant trip — at least for me. Maybe it would not be so nice at two in the morning. If you are at the age where you must make a nocturnal call, going outside is not so great. And I am told that in winter, in the rain, it is even less appealing.

This was to be our home for the next month. We were here for several reasons. One task was to continue with video editing projects. But we also hoped to assist the local fellowship in any way we could whilst here. Finally, we were there to test the waters to see if the Lord would confirm the leading to move here.

So Tülin faced the practical implications of living in an old, tiny stone house. For me, I enjoy the beauty, the history, the charm and delights of a stone courtyard house.

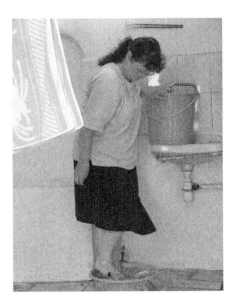

*Washing clothes...*

This was as far south in Turkey as we have ever been. The days were hot and the evenings/nights were remarkably cool. I, for one, do not 'enjoy' the heat. Nevertheless, I was able to work, albeit with a fan blowing on me. Having said that, Tülin found the heat quite unpleasant.

Ah, whilst writing this, I have been interrupted by the chiming of the bells of the local Orthodox church. This is definitely not a sound you will hear in most of Turkey. So, I will stop writing and continue in what the Lord has put in our hands to do. I'm editing and Tülin is washing clothes by hand and foot.

We press on 'continuing in what the Lord has given us to do'. Some-times it isn't very exciting, nor glamorous. It may be mundane, but if it is what the Lord has given us, then there is nothing more important for us to be involved in.

# 46

# October 2006 - 'Why Did You Tell Us That?'

H e looked across at me. He leaned forward and asked, 'Why did you tell *us* that?'

You know, when he asked me that question, I didn't know. I leaned back and asked myself, 'Why *DID* I tell *them* that?'

In the background, the women of the house busied themselves around the outdoor (tandoor) oven,[1] baking enough bread for a week to ten days. I was glad we were sitting in the shade of the olive trees. There, sipping Turkish tea from delicate tulip shaped clear glasses, we were chatting with the people we had come to see. We were in a village near Antakya. Here was a church consisting of believers from a Greek Orthodox background.

But I was troubled, even deeply disturbed, in my heart. Hence, I recounted my recent experience to these people. I was not seeking their comments or even an answer. I was sharing my difficulty in coming to terms with the experience and understanding of how I, as a believer, should respond to it. For days since it happened, it had been constantly in my thoughts. It rolled around and disturbed the thoughts in my mind. It was, literally, dominating my waking moments.

Let me tell you what had caused my discomfort. Hopefully, you will not join with these people and ask, 'Why are you telling me this?'

We had been in Antakya for about a month - this was our trial visit.

I was working on a video project while there. But we desired to serve the Church in any way we could. As the elder's wife and a Korean worker wanted to do some visits to a nearby city, we gladly provided the transport.

We left on a Saturday morning with two visits planned. It takes the best part of an hour to drive up the broad valley to where the road begins its tortuous path up the mountain towards the high pass – known in the Roman world as the 'Syriae Portae'(Syrian Gates).

The road was in good nick, but no matter how well a road is paved, a hairpin curve high up a mountain is still a hairpin curve. It is a long way up. Currently the road is composed of a downward lane, an upward lane, and a shared passing lane in the middle. It works, but it can be nerve racking.

A construction project was well advanced, providing a four-lane roadway up and over the pass. But a four-lane hairpin curve tight on the mountainside is still a hairpin curve that allows for no errors.

We crossed the summit of the pass and as we descended, the city of Iskenderun (ancient Alexandria) lay spread out before us. This city is but one of many named after its founder Alexander the Great. It is mute testimony to the rich and varied history of this area.

Our first visit of the day resulted from a contact via the Internet. It sounded promising, but it quickly became clear that the folks we were visiting had created their own personal version of faith, taking the bits they liked from Islam and adding their own customised bits. They were not open to hear the Good News, seeming quite content to work out their salvation according to their own desires and wishes. Many of the things they said and objections they raised were the old standard opinions and ideas concerning our Faith.

However, the Lord had brought several other people to that house on this occasion and one guest, a teenage girl, was more open, had sincere questions, and seemed willing to listen as well as to speak. So, we shared with her and trust the Lord that the seeds sown in that young heart would bear fruit. I happily made two trips back to the car to get books to give to those present.

On our departure, we asked for directions to where our second visit of the day would be. They looked at one another and gave directions, but they seemed uncomfortable. They asked why we were going there.

'We have another family we wish to visit.'

OK, but then they said that part of town was not very desirable. It was actually quite poor, with more crime. They wouldn't recommend we go. They were quite explicit, saying they would not go there. Nevertheless, they gave directions and off we went.

Now, initially, the directions were quite clear. But as we went further and further, it became harder to interpret what we remembered of the directions. After travelling quite a way, it was time to stop and ask for directions.

Now many men are reticent to stop and ask directions — that would include me. But I was vastly outnumbered in the car, three ladies to one man, and we had 'driven off the map' as far as the directions we had been given. So, I pulled over and directions were sought.

Hmm, we had driven past the area of town we were seeking and were indeed heading in the wrong direction. Then the debate. In Turkey you often encounter a debate about directions. If you ask more than one person - a debate is almost guaranteed. We asked two people and enjoyed an animated debate.

It seemed the best idea was not to go back the way we came and seek our missed turning. Rather, to go off in a totally new direction — with the caveat that once we had travelled for some distance, we would ask for more directions.

Now me, I would have preferred to take what little knowledge we had, i.e. the road we had just come on, and use that as a basis to find our destination. But we had asked for directions and the directions were to head off at a right angle to the way we had come and proceed 'up that road until it curves left and you turn right'. Okay...

So off we went, bumping and bouncing along, following the twists and turns of the road for an indeterminate time. After a while, it became clear to the majority in the car that it was time to ask for more directions.

Now the next chap we asked was a mini-bus driver. He knew his stuff and could get where he needed to go with no problem. But we were in an area where there were precious few street signs. Could he successfully communicate to us what we had to do to get where we were going?

So, after a description of curves, turns, bridges not crossed, and other vague and somewhat obscure instructions, we headed off.

Things went well until we came to the bridge. Now I thought we had all agreed that we were not to cross the bridge – but even on this we were not 100% agreed. The question was, 'Do we turn right or left?' Some were for left. One, I think, suggested we cross the bridge and then turn. I was for turning right. I was a minority of 'one', suggesting right, but as I had the steering wheel in my hands, I turned right.

Alas, there was a unanimous opinion among the majority. They felt, forcefully, that it was time to ask for directions once again. And so we proceeded along until we found someone to ask. We pulled up and made our inquiries.

As is the case most often when I have succumbed to the temptation to ask directions, this person didn't know the place we were going to. But at least they were honest about not knowing. Hence they were free to not give directions based upon a desire to help rather than on knowing where to send us.

So, no help there then.

Now the majority debated what the next move should be. Should we go on, go back, find another person to question, recross the bridge? While they engaged in the debate, I drove on in the direction I had chosen.

The houses fell away. On one side there was a fence and a field, and on the other side, a fence and a great man-made chasm for a motorway.

We proceeded between the two fences.

The murmurings from the back were not content nor encouraging. Finally, houses came into view and as we entered this part of town, the first business was to 'ask directions'. This was not an option, for the majority had spoken.

We stopped outside a house and the people were very helpful. The area of town we sought – well, we were in it. The street we sought, well, it was ahead on the right. We headed off full of confidence and encouraged.

We found the street and turned on it. I was not driving fast, as the elder's wife was looking for the house address. I passed an over-grown empty lot heading towards some more houses when a voice called out from the back seat, asking me to back up. I backed up and, behold, our destination *was* this overgrown empty lot.

I parked up. And, because of the fervent recommendations from our last visit, I locked the car.

We went up a little path between the wild bushes and a simple cinder block structure came into view. The loo was a 'long drop' near the road. In front of the cinder block structure – I hesitate calling it a house, for although it was being used as a house, a house it was not – there was a concrete slab that formed a kind of patio space.

The family came out of the shack to greet us; husband, wife and daughter. After handshakes and kissing cheeks, we assembled on the concrete space. Plastic chairs were found for most of us to sit on. The family reserved the stool and other simple items for themselves to perch on. After another round of asking after each other's health and again being welcomed, we began chatting together. Slowly, slowly, their situation unfolded before us.

The man of the house suffered from *Akdeniz Anemisi* or thalassaemia. This is an hereditary disorder of the blood causing anaemia. This is a debilitating disease for which there is no cure. This meant it was very difficult for him to find or keep work. Added to this was the fact that he had no trade or profession and just a basic education.

His wife was a quiet soul. She was the healthiest of the lot and had done cleaning and other manual jobs to provide some family income. Their daughter looked about nine, but in reality she was 12. She had inherited thalassaemia from her father.

And she had problems with her spleen and osteoporosis.

For reasons which were not clear to me, they had been abandoned by their greater family. They were truly alone. Before they were living in this cinder block structure, they were living in a field shrine.

This area is liberally dotted with these Shi'ite shrines where people go to pray, burn incense or make sacrifices. I have found a grave of a 'saint' or 'holy man' in all the shrines I have visited. I was surprised to learn that sometimes even Christian holy men are revered. These shrines can be in fields, mountains, towns and cities but predominantly are in areas with a high number of Shi'ite Muslims. *These shrines are anathema to Sunni Muslims.*

For over a year this family had no place to stay. So they lived in a shrine, the grave of the Saint, and received aid from those who came to pray. They had no water, electricity or sanitary provision, but they had no other place to stay. Now they had upgraded to this cinder block structure, which, at least, didn't contain a grave.

As we chatted, my attention was drawn to the small clowder of cats around the structure. I commented on the cats and they cheerfully told me that the cats were nice to have around as they kept the snakes away. They were not pets, and they did not feed them, but they were guard cats to ward off snakes!

The time had come, as part of traditional Turkish hospitality, to offer us, the guests, some fruit. An old plastic patio-type table was extracted from the part of the cinder block structure that served as a makeshift kitchen and was brought out to where we were sitting. Shortly thereafter, plates of fruit were placed before us. The fruit came from local trees, vines and from neighbours. I felt humbled by their generosity in the face of abject poverty, and I had to force myself to overcome my deep reticence in eating what little food they had. Tülin, feeling the same and knowing my thoughts, split an apple with me and we slowly consumed that and gave our thanks to our hosts.

It was almost school time, but the daughter would not be returning to school this autumn. She was bright, very intelligent indeed, but her health was a hindrance. The family was so poor that they qualified for free state medical treatment. The doctors wanted to do some tests to see if she could be helped by an operation. So, they would go to a hospital in Adana, a two-hour bus journey away. If she needed an operation, then that would be in Ankara, the capital, about eight hours away by coach. The test she would go to Adana to undergo was in the week before school began. Maybe after that she could go to school. She wanted to.

The medical care was covered by the State, but the travel to the hospital and other expenses were not. I heard not a word of complaint or despair.

The cinder block structure was roofed with corrugated iron. In summer it was an intense solar oven – in winter an impossible-to-heat icebox. They were not renting the structure – they were living in it. They had no rights. The owners could come and move them off the land at will. The property was an inheritance and the beneficiaries could not agree what to do with it. In this confusion the family had lived on the land.

Let me be clear: they were NOT a beneficiary. When the owners of the property sorted out their problems and decided what they wanted to do with the land, the family would have to move on.

After fruit came drinks. Thankfully, we had brought some soft drinks with us and so this was shared. After drinks came food. At this we drew the line. We really did not want anything to eat.

The man of the house and the daughter had made a profession of faith. The wife had not. In such abject poverty and hopelessness was their faith real, or were they reaching out for any help they could get? The Lord knows.

This I know: at no point did they ask for help, nor did they parade their need, nor did they hint or suggest how one might assist them. They never spoke of their need or of despair. Their clothes were clean, and they smiled, and their demeanour was pleasant.

We had a friendly conversation. They executed their duties as Turkish hosts very well. At the end of the visit, we prayed with them.

The spectre of a verse kept trying to burst upon my thoughts. Maybe you know the feeling, you 'know' the verse, but can't recall it word for word. I was having trouble finding it. And then it distilled in my mind. It says,

> 'If anyone has material possessions and sees a brother or sister in need but has no pity on them, how can the love of God be in that person?'

> 1 John 3:17 NIVUK

Life, in practice, is not simple. I wrestled with what I saw. I wrestled with what my response should be. I have 'this world's goods' and I had 'seen' with my own eyes, not been told, not been manipulated, not been convinced – no, but I had 'seen' with my own eyes a family in need.

But how can one help? If I reach into my pocket and pull out some cash and thrust it into their hands – what would be the result? Would they understand it comes from God who is greater than us all, or would they see me as a 'rich foreigner' and the 'source of aid'? What of the proverb,

> 'Give a man a fish and you feed him for a day. Teach a man to fish and you feed him for a lifetime.'
>
> Chinese proverb

Alas, this was what I shared with the people at the start of this story. I was trying to deal with what I had seen and the situation that I encountered. It was after I got it all off my chest that the man leaned forward and asked me, 'Why did you tell *us* that?'

One person listening to my account responded by telling a long story about how a chap had come to their fellowship, said the bailiff was coming to take all their family's household goods, and could the saints help. They did help and never saw him again. It seemed to me to be saying, *'Yes, we should help, but, unfortunately, because of the liars and charlatans in the world, we can't.'* That may not have been his message, but that is what I felt he was saying.

The fellow we were actually visiting, was one the elders of the church in this village outside of Antakya. He began by saying that the bulk of the people in the fellowship were day workers. They went out at the start of the day and hoped to find a manual day job. They worked and were paid for that day's labour. They were living on something between ₺300 and ₺350 a month (with no guarantee they would find work on any day).

Let me translate that into currencies you may find easier to understand: ₺300 = $228 CDN, $201 USD or £108; ₺350 = $266 CDN, $235 USD or £126 a month – as per the exchange rate in 2006. If you asked me if it were possible to live on such an income in Turkey, even rural Turkey, I would say no. Knowing the cost of living, it was remarkable to me that people were actually 'living' on that kind of income.

His point was the bulk of the people in the fellowship were living in poverty. He pointed out many were no better off than the situation I had described.

∾

After we returned to Istanbul, I asked to see the elder at the fellowship we are part of. The Lord also arranged it so another brother, whom I esteem, was also there and we discussed this whole question of how can we help those in need.

It became abundantly clear that it is not a new question or a straightforward question to answer. The elder lowered his head and with sadness spoke of gifts that resulted in more harm and *no good*. Let me explain that strange form of words: it was not more harm than good but, he explained, too often more harm and '*no*' good at all.

The elder shared from James:

> 'Suppose a brother or a sister is without clothes and daily food. If one of you says to them, 'Go in peace; keep warm and well fed,' but does nothing about their physical needs, what good is it? In the same way, faith by itself, if it is not accompanied by action, is dead.'

> James 2:15-17 NIVUK

Basically, he said, it came down to the most basic 'needs' – food and warmth (clothing). To this, we should respond without concern.

Everything else required wisdom and care. He added it was clear from experience, where possible, if the need was material, to give the material that was required. It was best not to provide money. If someone needed food, then give food; if they needed shoes, then give shoes.

We also discussed how it was important that people who are helped do not see the human agent – those whom God used to meet a need. It was best when they seek the Lord to meet their need and when it was met, rejoice and give thanks to the Lord.

The conclusion of our discussion was that we must respond to the promptings of God when we see needs. But in Turkey we must be very careful. We need wisdom to respond in a way that is truly honouring to the Lord. We want to be partners with Him in the Good Works He has prepared for us to do.

Maybe you are wondering, 'Why did you tell this story *here*?' Well, this time I know why I have recounted this experience. It is to share some of my struggle in this area of life.

I have been deeply moved and shaken by these events. God has given me of this world's goods and I have far more than ₺350 to live on in a month. I have no outstanding 'basic' need. I am well fed, well clothed, and with good housing. But, as the elder shared, any giving, any help, needs to encourage the saints in their walk with the Lord. It must aid their understanding of His love and His ability to provide for them.

Any action that any of us may engage in must do good and not harm our brothers and sisters in the Lord. As God has liberally blessed and provided for us, so too, we need to emulate Him and be liberally generous to those we meet. This is especially true for those whose basic needs we see.

# 47

# October 2006 - A Lesson
## there methinks

W e were in the *pearl of the Aegean*, the city of Izmir. Tülin and I travelled and stayed in the city for two weeks every month for over a year.

*The agora in ancient Symra - now Izmir*

This city was built over the ruins of ancient Smyrna[1] and it sprawls over an extensive area. Our friends lived in a place called Balçova[2]. It is noted for its hot springs. In fact, the thermal water is extremely abundant. The local council uses it to heat homes and apartment buildings.

This, I found, to be magnificent, I mean, imagine free heating and free hot water (!) with no carbon footprint in creating it. The hot water just freely comes up out of the ground. Of course, it isn't 'free'. To distribute the hot water, you need thermal lined pipes throughout the neighbourhood. To access the 'free' hot water, you have to pay a fee.

At the same time, I found this to be rather terrifying. After all, what is heating this 'free' hot water? Is it not molten rock? Solid rock that has become so hot, it has melted. And this hot, melted rock is very near. In fact, I would say the liquid rocks were unnaturally near - in fact, just under our feet.

But the one advantage of staying there was that we could visit the thermal springs. It was a real treat to indulge and relax in the natural hot water.

Hot springs are a draw - even an international draw. Hence, it was not surprising that many signs in the hot springs were bi-lingual. The signs were in Turkish and English.

Once, as I was passing through the lobby, my eyes fell on a rather large notice. Typically, the English drew me. I read that 'parents are liable from their children' and I must admit this tickled my funny bone. I snickered to myself over the obvious error. My assumption being it was supposed to be '*for* their children' but had been misspelled as 'from'. No doubt the sign-writer did not know suffi-cient English and so this error silently passed by.

Feeling smug, I then turned my attention to the original Turkish. But, I confess, when I read the Turkish, it surprised me. Let me explain. Turkish is a suffix-based language. This means suffixes are added on to words, and so, if we translate the notice, it literally is: 'parents children-your-from responsible [are]'.

When I read the Turkish, I knew straight away the source of my problem. The Turkish syntax showed the relationship between the noun 'children' and the adjective 'responsible'. This was done by using the suffix '*dan*'. So far, so good, but the problem arose in the translation of this Turkish - we typically render the suffix 'dan' as 'from' in English. The problem was not in the Turkish. The translator translated the Turkish into English - but they did it 'literally'. His English reflected Turkish syntax. It was written in English and yet, not fully English.

Another thing that struck me was that I would constantly translate this notice 'wrongly'. I would eschew 'from' and consistently use 'for'. The Turkish for 'for' is '*için*[3]', which is not a suffix but a separate word.

Oph! I made a rapid descent from smugness to chagrin. One moment I felt superior and the next embarrassment. My Turkish, which I speak with reckless abandon, reflects English forms and English syntax.

I had giggled when I read the English. That was wrong. If, in like fashion, Turks chuckled at my linguistic faux pas, they would be justified and smiling all the time.

But there is a problem. We have lived amongst Turks for thirty-five plus years. In that time, I've *never* overheard Turks mocking or laughing at our foreign linguistic faux pas - and we make some real bloopers. I have heard of many foreigners' gaffes. Some of which strike me as rather funny. And I have heard foreigners telling the tales.

But I've never heard the Turks 'telling the tales' of foreigners' bad Turkish.

I am ashamed to say I have made fun of someone's struggles in English. And I have witnessed other foreigners mocking someone's struggles in English.

I have found the Turks to be genuinely gracious. They strive to understand what the foreigner is trying to say. Full stop. They do not take the mickey out of foreigners, nor do they take pleasure at their expense. Here, I dare say, many a foreigner, and many a Christian, can take a lesson from the Turks.

Oh, as for the grammar lesson… it is only this year I'm applying it to my Turkish. I, besides my linguistic faux pas, must add I'm a slow learner.

# 48

# December 2006 - 'Down into the Fog we Plunged'

The aircraft descended through the gloom in those minutes before the sun set completely. As it did so, I noticed the white blanket of fog pasted to the landscape. The valleys were filled and the hills were wee islands, sticking up above the uniform sea of white. Our airport, on elevated ground, was standing proud of the fog and we came straight in for our landing.

This was not the case at Heathrow. It is one of the world's busiest airports and the UK's largest. However, all flights to there were cancelled. But not to Luton, on the northern fringes of London. This airport was still open as it is built on higher ground. And, as an added advantage, it is near to Hemel Hempstead, our destination.

Our flight up from Turkey was uneventful. This was our first time flying with EasyJet - a discount airline. The ticket was an incredible bargain. We paid £61 for us to fly from Istanbul to the UK - uh, that is not £61 each, but £61 *total*! That is fantastic. The seats weren't comfortable. And to add injury to insult, the chap behind me had his knees in my back. There were soft drinks and sandwiches - but for sale. Nothing was complementary - but the tickets were cheap. Besides, 'complementary' simply means 'included in the price' - it is not free, we have prepaid for it on full-priced airlines.

Our youngest son and his girlfriend were there to meet us. He didn't park up as airport parking was £4 for ten minutes (!). Hm, if he parked for an hour that would be £24 and our flight from Istanbul was £30.50 each. So, they drove around the airport until we came out and met them. As he drove us to Hemel Hempstead to pick up our car, we left the heights where the airport was located and descended into the valley, and entered the fog.

You could see, oh, maybe 100 metres - but everything was blurry, out of focus and dark. The sky didn't exist. There was just a low white canopy hanging above us and then descending on all sides. We were travelling in a small bubble of limited visibility.

Fog or no fog, life goes on. The next day was my outing to the dentist. My dentist works in a village called 'Much Hadham'. Travelling up to my appointment, we sailed on in the white sea that stubbornly lay over the land. In the country, trees and hedgerows rose out of the fog and dissolved as we twisted and turned our way to the village. Nothing was distinct. Nothing was clear. Nothing was in focus. The edges were blurred by wisps of white as the fog drifted and flowed around objects. It felt morbid, sad and hopeless.

After my check-up, with my teeth feeling bright and clean, we headed back into the fog. Time, it seemed, had ceased to have meaning. Every bend revealed either a white wall or yet another disappearing bend peering out of the fog. The road continued its serpentine path. This road was clearly *not* laid down by the Romans. In contrast to a Roman straight road, this road seemed to follow the path of a donkey tormented by flies and driven helter-skelter across the landscape - it was anything except straight. We ploughed on, sometimes in complete loneliness. Sometimes other vehicles appeared out of the vapours, either to accompany us or to make a fleeting appearance. Then they disappeared once again, enveloped in the ever-cloaking whiteness, leaving no trace of their existence.

As we neared Hemel Hempstead, our path took us to higher ground. Suddenly, the fog vanished and we saw a radiant blue sky with the golden globe of the sun shining. We were in a different world. Here we were enveloped in a world of beauty, clarity and focus. Here was time, grace and wonder. It was great. Our spirits soared. A different realm was before us and in confidence, joy and delight we drove on.

We rounded the crest of the hill and descended into the valley where Hemel Hempstead lay. The sun was once again consumed in the all pervasive white mantle. Everything again became blurred and darkness descended. Once again, all became unclear, unfocused and morbid. Occasionally, I would catch a glimpse of the sun; this round orb in the swirling white mass above us. We could not quite discern a familiar shape, it remained unclear - it was dimmed and had no effect to remind us of what could be.

If only there was no fog. The fog drains your energy, drains your spirits, drains your soul. Time loses meaning. You query yourself - is it 3:00 in the afternoon or 9:00 at night. Who knows? It is impossible to know when everything looks the same. We yearn for the fog to lift and the sun to reign.

And this experience, for me, summarises what it is like in Turkey. People are going about their business. But things are dark, uncertain, unfocused - morbid. Their world is dominated by an all pervasive fog. This fog obscures, blurs, inhibits and hinders all in every way. We speak of sun, of blue sky, of colours, of clarity and focus. To the hearer it is like gibberish and gobbledygook. Their world is so different. Occasionally, some may glimpse the Son through the fog. But they do not recognise Him. They cannot understand the beauty and warmth and colour and delight that come in His presence.

Yes, we live in a fog currently in the UK - but it will pass. In our other 'home', in Turkey, an entire nation is living in a kind of fog. But this fog has lain on their land for generations. It lies stubbornly and persistently blurring and blinding. It saps the energy and life and hope from everyone. We seek to bring light into the fog and explain the wonder, the joy, the amazement of life minus the fog and in the Son.

∽

# Notes

## Foreword

1. "Children are a heritage from the Lord, offspring a reward from him. Like arrows in the hands of a warrior are children born in one's youth. Blessed is the man whose quiver is full of them. They will not be put to shame when they contend with their opponents in court."
Psalm 127:3-5 NIVUK

## 1. September 2002 - A Small Town

1. Turkish is a fully phonetic language. All letters have a single value that is verbalised every time. Hence, Selçuk, with the 'c' with a ',' means we pronounce the word as 'sel-chuk'.
I have chosen to maintain proper Turkish spelling throughout this book.
2. To see the full account of the travels of the Apostle Paul, please read the Book of Acts in the New Testament. Therein you will encounter the founding of the early church in Central Anatolia and the journeys of the Apostle Paul.

## 2. September 2002 - Getting Settled

1. Adana is a major city in the south and east of the country, not far from the Mediterranean Sea. It is on the Çukurova plain and on the banks of the Seyhan river. We lived there in the early 1980s.
2. 512 kilobits per second - by today's standards that is very slow. But in 2002 - that wasn't a bad speed.
3. 56 kilobits is by all definitions painfully slow.
4. In those days, files were smaller than what we handle today - but 1.2 megabytes was not a large file - even then.
5. Broadband is the term that marks the difference between dial-up access to the Internet and a faster standard. This began with ADSL and has improved from there.
6. We defined the speed of the processor, how much RAM to have, how many and the size of the hard drives.
7. UPS - Uninterruptible Power Supply. The device has batteries and filters the incoming mains power. If the mains power fails, the batteries continue to deliver power to the computer. This both protects the delicate computer components and it means you can save your work before you have to power down your computer.
8. 1 GHz today is laughable - but then it was not too shoddy at all.
9. Apple Macintosh computers were then considered the better platform for editing video.

10. OS is the Operating Systems. This was when Apple were transitioning from their old OS, 9.2 and moving to their new OS, 'X'.
11. To start the computer - the operating system tells the computer what to do - in this way either drive could be used to run the computer
12. Today we use USB to connect to our computers. But then there was a high speed connection called 'Firewire'. At that time, they were much faster than USB. It was the connection of choice for those dealing with video.

## 3. September 2002 - Our First Shoot

1. Otoban is Turkish from the German autobahn.
2. St John the Evangelist Church - Photo: By A.Savin - Own work, CC BY-SA 3.0, https://commons.wikimedia.org/wiki/File:TR_Izmir_asv2020-02_img24_St-John_the_Evangelist_Church.jpg
3. A mark of the time. No video projector - just and old-fashioned overhead projector. You may need to look that up in Wikipedia.
4. 'You are the salt of the earth. But if the salt loses its saltiness, how can it be made salty again? It is no longer good for anything, except to be thrown out and trampled underfoot.'
   Matthew 5:13 NIVUK

## 4. October 2002 - Landlocked Dolphins

1. An agora, in Roman times, was a open market place. They were the commercial heart of the city. And, they were essential meeting places.
2. "For God so loved the world that he gave his one and only Son, that whoever believes in him shall not perish but have eternal life."
   John 3:16 NIVUK
3. "The thief comes only to steal and kill and destroy; I have come that they may have life, and have it to the full."
   John 10:10 NIVUK
4. "Taste and see that the Lord is good; blessed is the one who takes refuge in him."
   Psalm 34:8 NIVUK

## 7. April 2003 - A Castle, A Climb, A Turtle and a Twist

1. Turkish, pronounced a-la-shey-here

## 9. August 2003 - A Baptism in the English Channel

1. Çare - is a Turkish word, the first letter Ç is made up of a C and a ¸. In Turkish this makes the sound 'ch'. The word Çare means remedy or cure, and it looks like the English word 'Care'.
2. We were staying in Hemel Hempstead at the time

## 11. November 2003 - Shopping - Alaturka

1. "Let no debt remain outstanding, except the continuing debt to love one another, for whoever loves others has fulfilled the law."
   Romans 13:8 NIVUK

## 12. November 2003 - My Eyes Focused Slowly

1. Bostancı, like all Turkish words, are pronounced phonetically. When the letter 'i' (dotted 'i') is encountered, it is pronounced 'ee'. But when the letter 'ı' (undotted 'I') is read, it is pronounced as 'uh' - a sound in the back of the mouth.
2. A children's fun fair with rides and stalls

## 16. February 2004 - Ooops

1. Again, in Turkish, this is tohp-ka-puh - the last letter has a 'uh' and not an English 'ee' sound.
2. Literally this means 'filled-in garden' — land was created on the banks of the Bosphorus to house the palace.
3. This Turkish word, kadı (Kah -duh) means a Islamic judge, and Köy means village. In ancient times it was called Chalcedon, and now Kadıköy.
4. Haydarpaşa, pronounced Haydar Pasha is the name of the main train station on the Asian side of Istanbul. Haydar is a man's name and Paşa is a rank like general or admiral.

## 17. March 2004 - Unseen Forces

1. In Turkish the s with a ˌ under it is ş and is pronounced sh so this is Beshiktash - meaning cradle (beşik) rock (taş).

## 20. June 2004 - To Queue or not to Queue - There is no Question

1. Eminönü (em-in-on-u) is the area of Istanbul on the ancient peninsula and bordering the Golden Horn. As the ferries dock there, it is a major transportation hub.
2. Yusuf Paşa (pronounced Yu-suf Pa-sha) is an area in Istanbul on the ancient peninsula.
3. Emniyet (em-nee-yet) is an area of Istanbul. The name means security - and this is where the main police centre is located.
4. Dilekçe is pronounced di-lek-che

## 21. August 2004 - Reflections in the Water

1. Izmir (iz-meer) is a Turkish city on the Aegean Sea. Known in ancient times as Smyrna. It is described as the Pearl of the Aegean.

## 22. September 2004 - It Was a Very Reasonable Desire

1. Kabataş (ka-ba-tash) is on the European side of the Bosphorus.
2. The Princes' Islands - Photo: By Elelicht - Own work, CC BY-SA 3.0, https://commons.wikimedia.org/w/index.php?curid=22758626
3. Turkish meaning phaetons - pronounced fay-ton

## 26. May 2005 - Of Churches and Churches

1. Nevşehir (Nev-she-hear) is located in central Anatolia. The trip takes over 8 ½ hours, and is 447 miles in length.
2. Aramean = Aramaean
     This people group is called 'Suriyani' in Turkish and refers to an ancient Aramaic-speaking people.
3. This conference was organised by and for the ladies in the southeast region of Turkey.

## 27. June 2005 - The Journey of a Lifetime

1. Kuşadası ( kush-a-da-suh) is a town on the shores of the Aegean Sea. Its name literally means 'bird-island'
2. Pythagoreio - yes, Pythagoras lived on Samos (c. 570 – c. 495 BC).
3. PIM = Personal Information Manager - in this case it looked like a very small laptop with a grey screen and a keyboard.

## 29. June 2005 - Over the Hills and Dales

1. It seems every Romano-Greek town had an acropolis. Normally we think of one particular acropolis, in Athens, but it was by no means unique. They form a key part of the cities in this part of the ancient world.

## 32. March 2006 - Flip...Flap... Flutter

1. Eastern-style cushioned benches in a corner

## 33. March 2006 - If Not Here... Then There

1.  The term 'Noter' (pronounced 'no-tair') is the Turkish for a Notary Public. A Notary Public performs a necessary service in all forms of business. Many diverse documents must be notarised to complete even basic transactions. This is an essential form of income for the Turkish State.

## 34. April 2006 - Computers Make Life Easier

1.  A blue screen is the precursor to the now ubiquitous green screen. Whether blue or green, the screen is used to replace the fixed colour with a different background - ala Star Wars, a green screen changes the sound stage into a Star ship.
2.  The Blue Screen of Death occurs when the screen turns a certain shade of blue. It is frozen and does not function. When you see this screen it means Windows is in the terminal throes of a software crash. It is never a welcome sight.

## 35. April 2006 - In Search of a Good Restaurant

1.  Toros is Turkish. The English rendition of the name of the mountain range is Taurus.
2.  In Turkish pronounced pee-day
3.  Pronounced ja-juk. There is a similar dish in Greek cuisine called tzatziki.
4.  babaganuş pronounced ba-ba-ga-nush.
5.  Pronounced nar-ek-she-see.

## 37. April 2006 - Ah, the City of Urfa - Ancient Edessa

1.  Şanlıurfa, pronounced shan-luh-ur-fa.
2.  The city formerly called Urfa was renamed Şanlıurfa at the end of the war of Independence in the aftermath of the end of World War I. Many cities were renamed to reflect their contribution in the struggle to establish the Republic of Turkey out of the ruins of the Ottoman Empire.
3.  Some scholars suggest that the Ur of the Chaldeas that Abraham went to was actually Urfa - the name Ur still retained in its modern name. Not all scholars agree and the current consensus is the Biblical Ur is found 1,300 kilometres to the south east.
4.  Sark odası is pronounced sark *(ark with an s in front)* o-da-suh.
5.  Like many places that were renamed after the War of Independence, Şanlıurfa is also known by its former name of Urfa.
6.  A Turkish *kilim* is a pileless floor covering. It is handwoven using tapestry techniques. I daresay, now many *kilims* are the product of some factory.

## 38. April 2006 - It Was - But It Isn't - And Yet There Is

1. Urfa (ur-fa) has also been mentioned by its formal and longer name Şanlıurfa (shan-luh-ur-fa - meaning glorious Urfa - it was renamed after the War of Independence)

## 39. April 2006 - The Cold Rushing Waters of the Tigris River

1. Mangal, pronounced mahn-gall, is a Turkish barbecue. In this case they were portable metal rectangular constructions with sides. The charcoal is laid in the bottom and the skewers are laid across on the side suspended over the charcoal.
2. A saz is a long-necked stringed instrument. It is of the lute family and originated in the Ottoman Empire. It is similar to the Greek bouzouki. In fact the bouzouki was brought from Turkey by Greek immigrants in the 19th century
3. Pronounced dar-boo-kah.
4. Zaza is an Indo-European language. The Zaza people are a minority in eastern Anatolia. They are mentioned in the Bible in the first book of 1 Chronicles 2:33.

## 40. April 2006 - Off to an Ancient Monastery

1. Midyat is pronounced mid-yacht
2. A filmstrip was, as the name implies, a continuous roll of images that you projected on a wall using a 'filmstrip projector'. For a presentation, often a 'cassette tape' would be played and on hearing a certain tone, the person operating the filmstrip projector would advance to the next image. In the days well before smart phones, it worked. You may want to look it up on the internet.
3. Ululation (/ juːljʊˈleɪʃən, ˌʌl-/ ),[1][2] from Latin *ululo*, is a long, wavering, high-pitched vocal sound resembling a howl with a trilling quality. It is produced by emitting a high pitched loud voice accompanied with a rapid back and forth movement of the tongue and the uvula.[3] - - from Wikipedia https://en.wikipedia.org/wiki/Ululation
4. In Christian churches with episcopal polity, the rank of metropolitan bishop, or simply metropolitan, pertains to the diocesan bishop or archbishop of a metropolis - from Wikipedia - https://en.wikipedia.org/wiki/Metropolitan_bishop
5. Wikimedia Commons - By Nevit Dilmen - Own work, CC BY-SA 3.0, https://commons.wikimedia.org/w/index.php?curid=3981183
6. Süriyani is the Turkish for the ancient Syrian Orthodox Church. It is pronounced su-ri-yahn-ii. For more information readers are encouraged to go to Wikipedia at: https://en.wikipedia.org/wiki/Syriac_Orthodox_Church.
7. Tur Abdin (Syriac: ܛܘܪ ܥܒܕܝܢ, romanized: Ṭur ʿAbdin;[1] Arabic: طُوْر عبدين; Latin: Turabdium) is a hilly region situated in southeast Turkey, including the eastern half of the Mardin Province, and Şırnak Province west of the Tigris, on the border with Syria and famed since Late Antiquity for its Christian monasteries on the border of the Roman Empire and the Sasanian Empire. The area is a low plateau in the Anti-Taurus Mountains stretching from Mardin in the west to the

Tigris in the east and delimited by the Mesopotamian plains to the south. The Tur Abdin is populated by more than 80 villages and nearly 70 monastery buildings and was mostly Syriac Orthodox until the early 20th century.[2] The earliest surviving Christian buildings date from the 6th century.[2] - from Wikipedia - https://en.wikipedia.org/wiki/Tur_Abdin

## 41. April 2006 - Uncle Yohanna

1. Dayro d-Mor Gabriel (Classical Syriac: ܕܝܪܐ ܕܡܪܝ ܓܒܪܐܝܠ; the *Monastery of Saint Gabriel*),[1] also known as Deyrulumur, is the oldest surviving Syriac Orthodox monastery in the world. It is located on the Tur Abdin plateau near Midyat in the Mardin Province in southeastern Turkey. Wikipedia https://en.wikipedia.org/wiki/Mor_Gabriel_Monastery
2. In Turkish the honorific generally comes after the name. So, in this case, it is Yuhanna Uncle.
3. We would visit the ancient Syrian Orthodox monastery of Daryülzafaran Manastırı - or in English (from the Süryani) Monastery of Saint Ananias. Wikipedia https://en.wikipedia.org/wiki/Mor_Hananyo_Monastery

## 42. May 2006 - Slip, Slide, and Away... Almost

1. Izmir is a modern Turkish city built over top of the ruins of ancient Smyrna of Roman times. Smyrna is mentioned in the Bible.
2. Selçuk is a modern Turkish town laying on and near the ruins of ancient Ephesus - a noteworthy city in Roman times. It too features in the Bible and a book of the Bible was addressed to the believers living in the city.
3. Keçi, which simply means goat in Turkish is pronounced keh-chi and the next word Kale (ka-lay) means castle

## 46. October 2006 - 'Why Did You Tell Us That?'

1. As described elsewhere in this book - these ubiquitous ovens are found all over Turkey. And when village folk migrate to the cities and towns, they often try to recreate the ovens - an activity which is not encouraged by the town councils.

## 47. October 2006 - A Lesson there methinks

1. Smyrna was a major city in the Roman world and was ideally situated on a sheltered bay of the Aegean Sea and at the terminus of the Persian Royal Road - a major trade route.
2. Pronounced bal-cho-va.
3. Pronounced ih-chin

Printed in Great Britain
by Amazon